The Gift of Caregiving

Beverly Kidder D.S.W.

DEDICATION

This little book is dedicated to Shirley, my mom, without whom I wouldn't have discovered the Gift of caregiving and to Tom, my husband and Daniel, my son, who helped make Shirley's last few years a gift through their loving caregiving.

CONTENTS

ACKNOWLEDGMENTS

I wish to thank Steve & Gary Barg for their inspiration in creating the Fearless Caregiver concept and helping me to become a strong caregiver.
Also, thank you to Donna Fedus who met with me regularly at Ikea and kept me working at the project when my energy and interest waned.

And, with all things written, I give praise to Margaret Petersson who encouraged all her supervisees to write about their experiences.

1 CARE GIVING

There are **61.6** million people in the United States who are family caregivers. If all the family caregivers stopped providing care and their services had to be replaced by paid caregivers, it's estimated that the cost of providing the same level of care would be $450 billion dollars (AARP 2011).

It's common to hear people say that Americans don't honor older adults; don't care for family members; the American family has disintegrated through selfishness. It's commonly believed that the majority of older adults and persons with disabilities live in institutional settings, receiving paid, long-term care services. In fact, most people live and die in the community, often in their own homes and sometimes in the homes of family members. Fewer than 09% of people live in long-term care facilities. Most people receive the care they need from family members within the family setting. Even when it happens that someone is placed in a long-term care facility, family caregiving responsibilities continue. Families remain active, essential elements in the social and emotional life of loved ones who require long-term care, and are often also providing "hands on" care such as feeding their relatives.

I became a caregiver for my mother at some point, although I cannot pinpoint the date. At one point she was helping me provide daycare for my son and living independently, on the 2nd floor of our three- family home and eventually she became totally dependent upon me and my husband Tom to meet all her needs.

The transition from caregiver to care recipient was gradual. There was no single, spectacular event that changed the game, no sudden illness, no accident. We just experienced a long, slow, steady decline in function, accompanied by an increase in demand for help meeting the needs of daily life. My mom, Shirley, was one of the most independent women I've ever met. When she was a young wife and mother, our neighbor, Carrie, an older woman, advised her to act a little less independent because "husbands will let you do anything you're capable of doing. They won't help you if you show them that you can do it yourself."

Shirley didn't heed that advice. She prided herself on not needing help from anyone, to accomplish anything. That attitude enabled her to achieve greater success than often would be predicted, but also caused her to experience much stress and strain. People not only described her as independent, but also hard headed and stubborn. In our time together as her caregiver I came to know, appreciate and resent, at times, these traits.

My mother had chronic, obstructive pulmonary disease, hypertension and an enlarged heart. As she aged, each of these diseases got progressively worse, limiting her ability to maintain herself independently.

The changes were gradual and she compensated for the progressive loss of function by limiting her activities, thereby reducing the strain on her failing body. However, the more she limited herself, the more sedentary she became, the less strength she had. As a result, she had to further reduce *her activities. It was a vicious cycle. The less she did, the less she was able to do, but if she tried to do more she became so exhausted by the effort, she would collapse and be unable to do anything for days.*

I think back and try to recall when the decline began. I can picture her in the backyard teaching my son how to swing a baseball bat. She was fine then. I see her playing "cars" at the dining room table, surrounded by dozens of "Hot Wheels" and trucks, racing cars and letting my son, Daniel win every race. She was fine then. I see her waiting for the school bus to drop him off at the end of the day. Maybe she'd begun her decline by then. Initially, she waited at the bus stop, but eventually she waited at the window. The climb up and down the stairs was too much. It seemed like a small thing at the time, but maybe it signaled the beginning of the transition.

It was followed by her decision not to go to the super market for groceries, but instead, to give the list to Tom. Again, the stairs were a challenge. Tom, Daniel and I lived on the 1st floor and she lived on the second in an identical apartment. As the stairs became an increasing barrier, limiting time spent in the yard at cook outs, limiting opportunities to dine with us in my apartment, reducing participation at church and reducing trips to eat out. I offered to switch apartments; move to the first floor and continue the usual activities.

*But, the stubbornness kicked in,
"No!   I   don't   want   to
inconvenience anyone . I don't
want to live on the first floor,
someone might come in through
the window. I don't want noisy
people   (Tom   &   Daniel)
stomping   around,   over   my
head." There was no swaying
her. When she set her mind to
something,   she   was
immoveable."*

*During the last year of her life,
she never left the apartment
until she went by ambulance to
the hospital. By that time, all of
her needs were being met by our
caregiving " team".*

*Why is it that there is such distortion
between the reality of family
caregiving in this country and the
impressions of so many people?*

There are several factors that influence public perception of caregiving and have brought the issue into the public arena for discussion. One is the size of the population. There are so many people living in the United States today that even when the percentage of the population affected by an issue remains constant, the sheer number of the affected group is staggering, so we hear about it more often. Second is the aging of the population. We are living longer, much longer than our grandparents and more than twice as long as the founding fathers of this country.

In 1911, when an aging woman (60 something) needed caregiving, she would receive it from her daughter (40 something). In 1811, when an aging woman (40- something) needed caregiving, she would receive it from her daughter (20- something). In 2011, when an aging woman needs care (85+ something) she

*receives it from her daughter (65+ something).
Mothers, daughters and caregiving relationships
haven't changed. Just the ages of the care
recipient and the caregiver have added new
dimensions to caregiving.*

As we live longer and longer we
confront physical changes that we
escaped with shorter life spans. The
degree of orthopedic disability, the pain
and limitations caused by arthritic
conditions, the weakness associated with
chronic pulmonary and cardiac disease
result in care recipients who require a
greater degree of physical care than
would have been required in another
era. Also, the person providing the care
may no longer be young and free from
physical challenges associated with
aging.

My mother didn't provide care for her mother in the last stage of life. Shirley wasn't around at the time that her mother was aging and ailing, but she did provide care for both of her parents throughout their lives.

Shirley didn't graduate from high school-something that impacted her self-image and behavior throughout her life. Even in her late 80s she referenced that fact that her years of reading compensated sufficiently to hold her own in conversations with well- educated people; she was correct but she didn't really believe it. She was proud that I had completed my doctoral education, but she also dripped with sarcasm when she talked with me about it. She loved making comments like "book smart, not street smart" when describing Tom and me. The reason she didn't graduate and go on to pursue a nursing education, as she planned, was because her mother was very ill during Shirley's senior year and her father said she had to drop out of school and stay home and care for her. She could re-enter school the following year when, presumably, her mother would be well. After a year of absence from high school, and her friends all graduated, she never went back. She got a summer job at Woolworth's 5&10 cent store, working on the soda fountain. Summer turned to fall and she stayed on at Woolworth's. That year of caregiving for her mom was the first of several care giving experiences that left her feeling entitled to be the recipient of care later in her life.

When she was a young bride her father was diagnosed with severe heart disease. She went every day to her parents' home to help her mother *with caregiving. She stopped working, even though she and my dad were trying so hard to save up a down payment to buy a home. The caregiving needs of her father were more important to her than becoming a home owner. She made herself available when her siblings couldn't/wouldn't. She continued to help her mother provide daily care for many months. When her father's illness progressed to the point that he required hospitalization, she moved into his hospital room. She and her older sister and my dad divided the days into three shifts and one of them was there at all times so he'd never be alone or totally dependent upon paid caregivers. This caregiving experience also fed the notion that she was entitled to her share of caregiving when the time care.*

About 15 years later, she and my

dad relocated the family to California to start life anew. At the time, California seemed like the land of golden opportunity. They packed everything they owned into an old truck and the family into a newly purchased, second hand, blue Oldsmobile and we headed out in a caravan with another family to reinvent ourselves in California.

We were there about 5 months. The kids were all enrolled in schools and she found a job. My dad was working in a small machine shop started by the other family with whom we relocated. We were renting a small house in Spring Valley. Things were looking up, and then she got a call that her mother was ill and needed someone to stay with her. Although grandma lived with her adult, divorced daughter and her adult son, they never considered leaving their jobs to care for their mother; nor did any of the many other siblings, all of whom were living in the same town as grandma. No, the family expectation was that Shirley would quit her job and return, 3,000 miles, to Connecticut to care for Mama.

She took the kids out of school, bought tickets on a Greyhound bus, told my dad to call often, and she returned to Connecticut to care for her mother. Fortunately, grandma recovered and went on to live several more years. Ironically, in her final illness, Shirley wasn't available to care for her and that fact caused Shirley grief and guilt for the rest of her life. The guilt pushed her to even greater caregiver responsibilities in life.

Her older sister, Gladys lived in senior housing, one floor below Shirley. As she aged she became increasingly demented. But as is usually the case it wasn't a sudden, dramatic decline. At one point she was living independently in senior housing, shopping, cooking, making friends, celebrating holidays, and at another point in time, she didn't even know it was a holiday. If you didn't sit with her and encourage every bite of food, she'd forget to eat.

She eventually went to a nursing home, but for about 1 ½ years, Shirley was expected to "keep an eye" on her. That entailed visiting her daily, shopping, laundry, housework and trying to get food into her. Sometimes Shirley cooked, sometimes she brought food in from the nearby luncheonette, trying to tempt her with a special taste or aroma. She even tried home delivered meals.

She felt she couldn't ever miss a day, so that meant no vacations.

Caregiving for her was always a 7 day per week job. Gladys had an emergency call system, but Shirley was the one who received the notifications. It seemed the call button was constantly pressed. She resisted the suggestion of the housing director, to move in with Gladys, but for the amount of time she spent in Gladys' apartment, she might as well have become a live-in caregiver.

Make no mistake, there were other relatives who loved Gladys and helped out. Gladys's sister in law, Helen did the major grocery shopping and Gladys's son visited regularly and provided the happiness in Gladys's life. But the daily grind, the worry about the future, the visits to the doctor's office, the emergency calls in the night, the meals and the personal care, that was all Shirley. She continued until she couldn't do it any longer. She called a family meeting and said "I can't do it any longer." I wasn't certain what she thought would happen, but I know what she wanted to happen. She wanted Gladys's son to step in with his wife and children and fill the role that she'd been playing.

It didn't happen that way. He assessed the situation, declared it unreasonable to expect Shirley to continue to bear the burden of caregiving. The situation was unsafe without Shirley's constant monitoring and intervention, therefore Gladys had to go to a nursing home! In a matter of days he located a bed at a facility close to Shirley's apartment. In a flash, Gladys was transitioned to institutional caregiving.

Gladys' son visited once, found it "depressing", and made the decision to "remember her as she was" and didn't ever visit again. Other relatives followed suit. "She doesn't even know who I am. What's the point of visiting?" was a frequently heard refrain. So, as if she was already dead, mostly everyone backed away from caregiving responsibilities for Gladys. Everyone, except Shirley. She visited every day at lunch time to feed Gladys and stayed until the dinner tray arrived and she fed her the evening meal. Seven days a week for almost 2 years.

And then, there was Stella. Stella was mom's aunt, the oldest living member of her family. She didn't even have a close relationship with my mother. Shirley always felt Stella looked down on her. Stella worked for the Grace Hospital School of Nursing which eventually became part of Yale University. She was a *housing manager in the dormitory. That was back in the day when young nursing students had to "dress" for dinner and their attire for a trip into town had to be approved by the housing manager. Properly dressed students wore a hat and gloves into town. Shirley felt Stella looked down on her because she failed to follow through on her plans to become a nurse. Whether Stella cared enough about her to even consider Shirley's future plans is unknown. In fact, there isn't any evidence to believe that Shirley's existence ever entered Stella's rarified atmosphere, until, Stella was a very old woman. Stella was 97 lived alone, had no children and no one to help her when she needed caregiving. She was hospitalized with an obstructed bowel and had surgery. Following the surgery, she needed personal care and assistance with activities of daily living until* she regained her strength. In the absence of family to provide care, the plan was for Stella to go to a nursing home. She was devastated and felt (probably correctly) that if she went in she'd probably never get out. There's so much that can go wrong at that late stage in life. She had never imagined not being able to live in her little efficiency apartment.

She cried out her woes to Shirley when she visited her one afternoon at the hospital. Although they were never close, Shirley felt that out of respect for her own mother, who was Stella's sister, that she should visit as a representative of the family. When Stella told her story, she tapped into Shirley's guilt about not being there to care for her mother in her last illness. She decided that it was her opportunity to assuage her guilt by caring for her mother's sister.

So, Stella went home to the tiny, one room efficiency apartment and Shirley went with her. She slept in the recliner and provided care 24/7. The Visiting Nurse came in, and monitored Stella's progress in recovery. She was a remarkably strong, independent woman. With care, attention and rehab services in her home, she made a full recovery. After 2 months, Shirley was free of the recliner and returned home. The pattern was now established however. Although Stella made a full recovery, she felt afraid to venture out alone, so Shirley went with her to her many doctors' appointments and she did the shopping for her. She also did the laundry because carrying the basket to the laundry room was too difficult for Stella after the surgery. Bit by bit activities were transferred from Stella to Shirley. Shirley was visiting 3 – times per week. They continued in that relationship for almost 2 years. As Stella approached 100 years, she became increasingly frail. Shirley's visits increased to daily and then one day Stella was very sick. Shirley called an ambulance and Stella died on the way to the hospital.

Caregiving, 100 years ago, was not primarily provided to advanced, elderly, chronically ill relatives. More often, it was care of acutely ill or terminally ill loved ones. The caregiving relationship was time limited. The average life expectancy was only 47 years. With more and more people living 100+ years, caregiving can become a lifetime commitment for the caregiver because we know that long-term caregivers do not enjoy the long life of the care recipient. Caregivers may die before the caregiving responsibility ends. In fact, for some caregivers, their own death may seem like the only relief they can accept from the caregiver role.

Third, even with degree of infirmity aside, caregiving today is more difficult because our lives have changed. In 1911, men were just beginning to work outside the family homestead, and women were firmly fixed at home, full-time, with very few exceptions. African-American women and newly arriving immigrant women worked in the homes of others but very few women were engaged in paid employment in the developing industrial era. As late as 1970, only 33% of women were in the work force. Fast forward to 2011 and women are expected to work outside the home and contribute financially to the family budget. Domestic arts alone do not support families in the 21st century. The standard of "need" has changed over time and the strains on the national economy have made it necessary for families to have two paychecks to meet basic needs, even as they were defined prior to cell phone bills, cable TV, 2 car families and fast food restaurants. The cost of basic housing, heat, food, transportation, laundry, clothing , education and health care, has increased to the point that without women working, for the first time in history, American families would experience a lesser quality of life than their ancestors enjoyed.

Although money is clearly a strong motivator for women to work outside the home, it isn't the only one. As society has opened the doors to women in education and employment , more and more women have found a sense of pride and accomplishment in work outside the home that has improved their sense of themselves and their place in the world.

The result of women working outside the home however has been an ever-increasing demand on women's time as they attempt to fulfill all the traditional roles and functions assigned to them by society and the new roles and demands placed on them in the workforce.

My father was a traditional man. Born in the 1920s, he had typical expectations of women based on roles that society promoted in that era. In real life he experienced women in non-traditional roles however. His mother was an equal, if not dominant partner in the family business. She worked every day in the family owned and operated grocery store. From early morning until late in the evening she unpacked boxes, shelved canned goods, sliced cold cuts in the deli, swept floors, pulled orders for delivery and in her spare time worked on the books. My grandfather waited on the customers. He had the charm and provided customer service. They were both integral components of a successful business.

Conveniently, the store occupied the first floor front portion of their multi-family home. The family lived behind and above the store. In addition to working 7 days per week, Grandma birthed and raised 6 children and became a relative caregiver for an orphaned cousin. The housewife role included all the responsibilities usually ascribed to women and mothers. There was no hired help to cook, clean, babysit or perform any of the other tasks involved in running a household and raising a family. As her daughters grew, they took on many of the family tasks, enabling grandma to spend even more time in the store.

Grandpa had his 1st heart attack at an early age. At the doctor's request, he cut back on time spent in the store. Grandma and the teenage kids filled in the gap. That was the model my dad knew and what he expected from women. Total commitment. Willingness to work 24/7. Self-sacrifice. He commanded no less from Shirley. My dad's health wasn't good. Although he looked strong and healthy, the doctors advised my mother that he wouldn't have a long life and would be plagued with health problems.

He managed to live decades longer than predicted but always contending with acute and chronic health problems. Many times, *throughout their complicated relationship, Shirley served as his caregiver. When I was 6 he became acutely ill and was hospitalized for many months. We were a very poor family, living in public, subsidized housing: the projects. They weren't pretty, but it was all we could afford. When my dad got sick, and was unable to work, there was no income. We had no way to pay the rent, so we were evicted from the projects. It's difficult to imagine being too poor to afford the projects, but we were.*

Eventually someone told my mother about the "welfare office". The state welfare office was unable to help us because we were an intact family with a "male, head of household", living with us. That made us ineligible for benefits. The state referred us to the city welfare office, who provided us with a rent voucher and a weekly food allowance of $10.00. Shirley found an apartment in a 6 story, walk up tenement, in a bad neighborhood and moved the family. She fed us pretty good meals on that pittance.

At the same time she took care of my father and nursed him, slowly back to health. She cooked and cleaned for all of us; nursed him, helped us with our homework and entertained my dad who was always in need of attention, storytelling and singing. Sometimes, she was the performer and sometimes she was the audience for his stories or songs. She saw it all as part of her role as caregiver for the family.

With money so limited she determined she couldn't survive on the charity of the city, so, like grandma, she began working. At *many points in our life she was the only wage earner and often she was the dominant earner. She brought every penny home and turned it over to my dad. He wasn't the best money manager, so we never advanced beyond abject poverty under his leadership, but she never challenged his authority as the titular head of the household. She saw her role as helpmeet and caregiver.*

The responsibilities of holding a job were added to the responsibilities of her traditional roles of wife, mother and daughter. There never was conversation about dividing the responsibilities differently or getting help from anyone else to meet the needs of the family. All the caregiving responsibilities were consigned to one person, without thought about the impact of those responsibilities on that one woman.

Common wisdom would lead you to believe that the increasing demands outside the family home on women have resulted in shifting roles between women and men. Men are more actively involved in parenting, household chores and family caregiving. Movie and TV programs showcase "stay at home" Dad, single-parent Dad, Dad doing the laundry, Dad helping solve the latest parenting crisis, but not even TV pretends that Dad is providing hands-on care to Grandma.

Studies of caregiving demonstrate that while there has been an increase in household activity by men and that men are more involved in family caregiving than they were in 1911, the percentage is still significantly less than the care provided by women. The caregiving tasks men have assumed are predominantly money management and home repair.

Women have moved *en masse* into the work place but they haven't left the family home, or the responsibility for ensuring the needs of family members are met. *How can women work outside the home 8 -10 hours per day and still attend to the needs of the family?* Research demonstrates this incredible feat is accomplished by completely ignoring their own needs.

Women have cut corners on their personal care, health care, recreation time, vacation, socialization, spiritual life, creative time and intimate time with loved ones. They haven't given up responsibility for parenting issues, food preparation, holiday celebrations, sick care, school participation, housework, laundry, shopping ……..and the list goes on. Rather, they have cut corners on how they do things: serve more packaged meals, send more store bought items to church bake sales, attend the school play but not volunteer to direct it, wash & dry the laundry but not get it into the bureau drawers and dust only when company is coming. The result is often a poor sense of self as a homemaker and mother and also, a poor sense of self as an employee when the demands of the job call for staying late and the pull of family requires leaving on time.

Shirley was a decent cook but she never claimed to cook like "Mama". Mama was her mother and a family legend in the kitchen. She could make heavenly dishes from any items found in her pantry.

Throughout the Great Depression, her family never realized how bad things were economically because in their home there were delicious meals with plenty of food to share with friends and neighbors who dropped by at dinner time. Shirley couldn't create magic meals without the ingredients to cook or the luxury of time to turn an inferior cut of meat into a tender, luscious treat. She worked with what she had in terms of time and money, and both were very scarce. This meant she used many short cuts, prepared foods and modern inventions to shorten meal preparation time. This was essential because after working all day she had to wait at the bus stop for a bus into town where she'd wait for another bus to travel home. Then she'd launch into dinner preparation,

dining and then homework, each of
us working on a different project
with different levels of interest and
ability. When homework was
completed, the baths and bed
preparation began. Little boys can
get dirtier in one day than anyone
can imagine. There were no nights
when the bath could be skipped.
After the baths, and settling everyone
down for sleep, Shirley returned to
the kitchen to wash the dishes and a
load of laundry in the old wringer
washer. The laundry remained in
the basket to be hung in the morning
before taking the bus to work. It was
a full challenging day and every short
cut helped immensely. Although she
used short cuts in cooking, she
wasn't proud of it, resenting
comparison to her mother.

My father wasn't an appreciative care recipient. He was, at times, mean in the way he "teased" Shirley about her culinary skills. One evening after Shirley put on a dinner of hot dogs and beans (from a can), my dad made a sarcastic comment about "another gourmet meal". She lost it. Her hot dog was all set to be bitten into: Guldens spicy mustard, relish and sauerkraut. She picked it up and hurled it at my dad, hitting him smack on the forehead. The sauerkraut spilled down onto his eye glass frames and the mustard dripped down his face. He sat there, calmly and asked " Why did you get so upset?" and proceeded to pick up his hot dog, bite it and rave about how delicious it was, all the time acting as if there was nothing unusual. The sight of him sitting there, eating, remains one of the most comical memories I have. Soon she was laughing and so were all the kids. Caregiver stress relief can come in many forms, a good laugh can help.

This is a common picture of the average, middle-aged, working mother. Add to this picture the needs of an aging parent or ailing spouse, who like everyone ever surveyed wants to remain at home and receive loving care from the already over-extended daughter!

2 THE BUCK STOPS HERE

As members of families we confront many instances when we declare "It's my turn!", often followed by "It isn't fair!". Whose turn is it to wash the dinner dishes? Whose turn is it to sit at the kids table on holidays? Whose turn is it to watch younger kids instead of playing with our own friends?

The decisions about whose turn it is are made, in many different ways and often reflect values and customs of different family cultures. In some families there's a genuine attempt to be fair in the assignment of family chores, in others, decisions are made with expedience in mind, and in some, culture and tradition alone are the prevailing determinants of labor distribution.

Many of the deciding factors are gender-based, even in 2011. As a society we are still working within male/female roles. Tasks within the family continue to be assigned based on gender. The loosening of gender-based roles has happened more on the periphery of society than in the family home. Sixty-five percent of family caregivers are female.

Even within a family who fights gender-based roles to allow a talented, athletic daughter to play ball on a traditional all-boys team, at home there is no comparable division of tasks based on skills and abilities. Rather, washing the dishes after dinner is automatically relegated to the daughters, whereas, taking out the trash is assigned to the sons. There is no consideration of the fact that the son is slight of build and has difficulty carrying heavy trash cans.

The decision about who should do what is most heavily tied to gender.

In addition to gender, in many families birth order plays a role in deciding whose turn it is when family chores are assigned. Different cultures do it differently but responsibilities and privileges often pertain to being oldest, first born son, baby of the family or last born after a decade of infertility. The family relationships, with each of these positions, is unique between siblings and between parent and child. Often, these relationship dynamics form the basis of lifelong determinations about roles within the family. Decisions about family matters continue to be made long after the relevant attributes of the person making the decisions have ceased to exist, and all that remains is the tradition within the family.

Shirley's mother, Mama, gave birth to 8 children, one of whom died in a tragic accident. He was struck by a trolley car on the street in front of their home as Mama looked on, helpless, out of the window in the front room of her home. She was, understandably, devastated by her loss. The message from grandpa, to Shirley was "Take care of your mother." Shirley was 9 years old. How does a 9 year old "take care" of a parent?

It isn't clear how she interpreted her responsibilities in that role, but what is clear, is that she took the responsibility seriously and experienced considerable guilt over the fact that her caregiving efforts weren't good enough to prevent serious depression in Mama.
She went through a few very difficult years developing addictions to tobacco and whiskey, which she

used to ease the pain she experienced. Part of Shirley's caregiving was to monitor Mama and try to keep her away from whiskey until as late in the day as possible. Instead of whiskey, she'd walk down the block to Hull's Brewery and buy a pail of beer to pacify Mama. If she could keep her away from whiskey until her father came home, that was considered a success.

Shirley's older siblings were married and out of the house so Shirley helped care for her 2 younger brothers, making sure they got out of bed and got ready for school; ate a donut before they left, changed out of their school uniforms after school; and most importantly, didn't upset Mama.

I remember a family I knew as a teenager. There were twin daughters my age who had an older brother. Tony, was charged with the responsibility of making certain the girls didn't get "into trouble". We were pretty tame, shy, gawky teens and there weren't a lot of offers to get "in trouble". Even if opportunity presented itself however, there was no way these girls were going to risk the wrath of Tony. He executed his role through power, intimidation and fear. He threatened them with bodily harm if they dared walk down a street he determined off-limits, and he threatened to beat any boy who spoke to them. Bigger, older and meaner than anyone else, everyone feared him and the girls obeyed him.

Fast forward forty years. The older brother is retired, has chronic lung disease making breathing very difficult. He relies on oxygen that he carries with him in a portable canister. The "girls" are in their mid-fifties. At a recent school reunion of their Catholic grammar school, a group of old friends decided to plan a weekend trip to New York City. They would see a play, go to Little Italy for dinner, shop and laugh like in the old days. And what do the sisters say when the plan is proposed? "We can't go, Tony would kill us. He doesn't approve of women going to New York alone. That's how they get "in trouble"."

How could Tony kill them? He can barely speak!!

Tony's need to keep the "girls" out of trouble is long over. They're married women, mothers, competent and independent in most instances, but not when it comes to challenging Tony. Can you imagine a day when the girls would stand up to Tony and tell him

they've decided to locate an assisted
living family for Mom and Dad because
they can't keep up with the work of
caring for them at home, caring for their
husbands and homes, helping babysit
for their grandkids and working fulltime
to help support their families? Do you
suppose Tony would say "We need to
find a solution that will work for
everyone. We can't sacrifice one life for
another. Let's discuss this." *I don't think
so.* Family tradition keeps old roles
alive.

As in most families, the responsibility
for caregiving will fall to one or two
members who are pre-selected by
culture, tradition, roles and
relationships. Is this a bad thing? Not
necessarily. It can be very comforting
to have a defined role within your family
and feel comfortable about your place
within the family. But sometimes roles

are based on power and abuse from early childhood relationships that is used to manipulate people as adults. Sometimes we change over the years and the role we played within the family at an earlier age no longer fits. Sometimes we lack the ability to keep on in the pre-selected role due to age, interest, infirmity or resources. At these moments, we need to re-examine our roles within the family and determine a "goodness of fit" between our needs and the needs of the family.

When Shirley was a mother of 5 children, newly relocated to California, trying to help establish her family in a new setting, she received a call from her family saying she was needed in her traditional role of caregiver for her ailing mother. She shouldn't have come back to Connecticut to care for her mother. She was in no position to assume the responsibility for her mother. The results of her choice lead to major changes in her life and the lives of the family she created through marriage and child bearing. At the moment when she had to choose between fulfilling the old role she'd been assigned in childhood and the life she'd made as an adult, she was torn between what was best for her husband and children and honoring the relationship and responsibilities she'd accepted throughout her life. She chose to honor the past. She couldn't see herself abandoning the role of caregiver, so she tried to convince herself that she could do it all. She could be a partner to her husband three thousand miles away. She could uproot her children and, relocate them without a plan. She had no home to bring us to, no *money to establish a home, no relatives welcoming us. Every possession we owned was left behind. She didn't know where we'd go to school or how we'd get money for food. She just knew she had to get home to care for her mother. Her father's imagined approval was an essential element in her decision. She knew that her late father would expect her to do as much for her mother as she had done for him. And so, she ignored the "goodness of fit" between her needs and the needs of her young family and she yielded to the old role she filled earlier in her life..*

If your role within the family is generally satisfying, and your capacity to fulfill the responsibilities of the role are sufficient; and you are the one who has the relationship with the person needing care within the family, then *the buck stops here!*

Having the relationship doesn't mean you are the closest, enjoy each other's company the most, or get along the best. In fact, it may be just the opposite. However, it means that in your relationship you are the one who has been pre-selected to sacrifice of yourself to meet the needs of this person. Beneath conflict, struggle over power, differences of opinion, there is basic trust between you and the person you care for. The trust enables him/her to turn part of his/her life, power and independence over to you, albeit with resistance and maybe even resentment. Why? Because they know the buck stops here, with you. You won't pass them on to someone else. Even when it gets really tough you can be trusted to care for him/her. Trust is the basis of our first relationships in life and is essential to maintaining a loving relationship throughout life. When we say, "I love you." We are saying "You can trust me. I have your back. I'll be there for you. The buck stops here."

Shirley helped care for her sister Betty. Betty was 10 years older than Shirley. She was prettier and favored by their father. She'd been a small, sickly, beautiful child who developed tuberculosis as a young woman and spent a year in a sanitarium during the TB epidemic in the 1940s. The disease left her with diminished lung capacity and she was plagued with chronic lung disease throughout her life. As a result, she was frail and commanded extra attention and caregiving throughout her life. Some of the time, Shirley provided that care.

When Betty was a young wife and mother, she was over-taxed by the strain and needed help. Her father made 12 year old Shirley move in with Betty to help with the care of her nephew and assist with household chores and shopping. Every day Shirley got up and did the morning errands and then went to school. After school she returned to Betty's apartment where she received instructions for shopping, taking clothes to the laundry or taking the baby for a walk, or any other chore Betty deemed necessary.

No one knows how much work Shirley was actually required to do; Betty and Shirley had different versions of those days, but they both concurred that Shirley couldn't go out and play with her friends or stay after school for activities, or have friends over to visit. If Shirley disobeyed, Betty called their father and he chastised Shirley. One other thing they both recalled was that Shirley wasn't allowed to go to sleep at night until Betty's husband, Bobby, came home from work. Bobby worked as a waiter and didn't typically return till midnight. Shirley had to remain awake, despite having to rise early in the morning to go to the store for fresh milk and bread from the bakery, before going to school, because Betty was afraid to be alone.

In retrospect, it's not surprising that Shirley expected me to sit with her throughout the night when she needed care and was afraid she might die alone, despite the fact that I had to go to work in the morning. That was part of the role of the caregiver as she lived it.

3 CONNECTED ETERNALLY

The difference between family & paid caregiving

I remember one time when my brother and I were having an argument over something silly. We each had an opinion and each was convinced it was the "right" opinion and the other was wrong. We were trying to prove our point and "win". As were pressed our respective points, we became more determined to win. As often happens with family "debates", voices were raised, volume increased and we were shouting at each other. Suddenly, he stopped talking and laughed. I looked at him, trying to figure out what was so funny. He said "you know what's really cool about fighting with you? No matter how mad we get at each other, we can't break up. It's not like fighting with my girlfriend; you're my sister for life!" There are so many instances when family members become angry with one another, in some cases the anger remains for years, but angry or not, they are still family.

It is the eternal connection between family members that enables us to rely on those relationships when we need help. We may not "deserve" help. We may not have earned the right to ask for or expect help from a family member, but in most cases, we will receive it. This is the reason why 97% of care is given by families. Not because 97% of all family members were in loving, mutually reciprocal relationships in which each member "paid their dues" and earned the right to expect care and attendance from relatives, but rather, because there is an eternal connection, based on love.

Betty and Shirley were together throughout their lives, not always harmoniously, but always there and interconnected. So, when Betty was old, and abandoned by her second husband who was 30 years younger than she, she turned to my mom to care for her. Over the years, Shirley and Betty totally disagreed about Betty's husband and they fought about him often. At the time he walked out on Betty, leaving her sick, bed ridden and alone, in an apartment, 1,500 miles away from her family, they weren't on speaking terms. They had had an argument about him during Shirley's last visit to Betty. But in the moment of crisis, Betty knew she could call Shirley to care for her and she'd be there for her. And, she was right. Shirley dropped everything; hopped on a plane and was by her side the next day. She helped care for her until she died, including arranging to transfer her, by train, back home to be with the family. Betty's son became the primary caregiver during that time but Shirley was there in the crisis and spent part of every day with her until the end. She knew their relationship was built on lifelong connections and that Shirley could be trusted.

Love within a family may not be readily apparent and may not be direct. One sibling may be caregiving for another because of a love relationship with a parent who uses that relationship to extract commitment to care for a needy sibling as a demonstration of love for the parent.

I recall a woman I knew who had three children, two daughters and a son. The son was born with severe developmental disabilities. The needs of the son were extensive, but the woman was determined she would raise him within the family, not utilizing institutional or professional care. Her responsibilities for his care were all consuming, leaving her no time or energy for the rest of the family. Eventually, her husband left the family. Her sister became the primary parent for the daughters. When the woman was in her sixties she developed cancer and was given a poor prognosis. She called in her daughters and made them promise to care for their brother forever. The daughters didn't have a strong relationship with their brother. In fact, they felt resentment toward him for having disrupted the family. They didn't want to care for him but, their desire to please their mother, and maintain a loving connection with her, lead them to agree to care for him for life. Even after her death, when there was no tangible connection to her, the daughters kept their promise.

Without the power of love, we wouldn't have family caregiving. It is only our emotional connection to the people for whom we care that keeps us on the job. Without love we can base our decisions on practical factors such as our physical and personal resources. We can ask ourselves what we'll get out of the caregiving relationship, not just what we'll put into it. In most things there is an obvious give and take in what we do. I pay my dues and expect to get something back in return. There is a social economy that guides our expectations. It's common to criticize someone who is "all taking and no giving". We have expectations throughout life that we give and we get. But the giving and the taking aren't always equal in a linear path.

Sometimes, as with infants, there's a lot of giving in the early phase before the baby can begin giving back. In family caregiving for adults, we may be benefiting from giving to the caregiver years before. The unknown, emotional elements in the complex relationships between family members are powerful, if often incomprehensible, motivators of caregivers.

There was a single parent family with six children. The mother was an alcoholic. At one period in the life of the family, four of the older children were taken away from the mother and placed in institutional care by the state child welfare department. The two younger children were left in the care of the mother. The older children remained in institutional care until age 18 and then went out on their own. Each fared reasonably well and made independent

lives, married and began their own
families. Throughout their adult lives
they rivaled each other in their efforts to
win the favor of the mother. They
bought expensive gifts for her, vied with
one another to entertain her on holidays
and take her with them on family
vacations. As she aged, they became
family caregivers. They provided
incredible care to this woman with
severe chronic lung disease, who
required constant oxygen and
pulmonary suctioning multiple times
each day.

The connection between the siblings
and with the mother was the powerful,
unbreakable basis for caregiving. The
rewards to the caregivers were
emotional, not tangible and could not be
quantified. Contrast this with paid

caregiving which is easily quantified. If caregiving costs $18 per hour, for $72 you can receive 4 hours of care. If you spend $63 on care, you'll receive a half hour less care, and if you spend $81 you'll get a half hour more care. Paid caregiving is based solely on economics. Although companies that provide caregiving often present themselves as 'loving", "caring" providers of care in "family like" settings, it's important to recognize that the caregiving relationship isn't based on love and eternal connections, but on money. Proof of this is readily apparent. Stop paying the professional caregivers and see how many hours of uncompensated care will be provided. Call an agency and ask them to send a caregiver to help care for your mom and tell them "Oh, by the way, I won't be paying for the service." They won't come.

While there are some non-profit caregiving organizations which may provide care at no-cost to you, that doesn't mean that there isn't a charge for the care and an economic basis for the relationship. Perhaps a grant or foundation is paying for the services provided. Someone is paying the coordinator who is setting up the plan and someone is paying the person providing the service.

There are some non-profit, caregiving organizations at which the caregivers are volunteers. No one pays them for the service they provide. Many of these organizations are tied to churches. The care they provide is based on love, but not based on a direct relationship with the care recipient, but on a love relationship with God which is demonstrated by the caregivers serving another "child of God". Although the caregiving in this relationship is important and can be a powerful benefit to care recipients, it is extremely rare that the care provided includes accepting responsibility for the care recipient, including making decisions about care needs. So, even with love in the equation, there remains a basic difference between care provided by family and care provided by organizations.

Relationships based on economic formulae, meted out based on the capacity of the organization to meet needs and the financial resources of the care recipient to pay for care, are different in nature, commitment, duration and responsibility from family-love based relationships. There is no end to the family connection. When a family care recipient is unreasonable, irrational, uncooperative, unwilling to accept needed services, unwilling to buy needed equipment, the paid caregiving organization can pull out. They can assess the situation as "unsafe" and refuse to participate in an unsafe situation. When the visiting nurse, the home health agency, the home equipment supplier leaves the "unsafe" situation, the family caregiver is left to care for the care recipient. Unsafe, safe, easy, difficult, gratifying or distressful, the caregiving need and relationship between family caregiver and recipient is eternal.

When Shirley was near the end of her journey, she was unreasonable and very difficult to satisfy. She became completely bedridden and could not be left alone when I was at work. I had to continue working, so we needed to find someone to come in and sit with her a few hours each afternoon before Daniel got home from school. Although she was eligible for assistance from community agencies that provided in-home care, she refused to accept services from them. The fact that I worked at an agency that provides homecare, meant nothing to her. She didn't want any "nosy strangers" in her home. I found an independent provider of homecare, who came highly recommended, but she rejected her for no apparent reason. I was at my wits end, and I knew we were in a dance and she was leading, but I couldn't continue dancing to her tune. I had to get back to work. She recognized this, got on the phone and hired Sonia, the mother of her brother's cleaning lady. She came 4 hours a day to fix lunch, help mom to the commode and sit with her in the bedroom. The fact that this woman only spoke Spanish didn't strike my mom as *problematic.* She determined that she'd use the time to learn Spanish and teach Sonia English.

And so began our cultural adventure. It was great the first week or two. Marguerite, Uncle Bill's cleaning lady and daughter of Sonia was in frequent phone contact with her mom and me. We were all happy. Sonia was cooking new, ethnic dishes for Shirley. A cloud seemed to lift at home. Maybe we were on a path that would help us settle in and get some normalcy back into the household. But, no... about 2 weeks into the plan Shirley started to complain that the food was not agreeing with her, that Sonia only wanted to watch Telemundo T.V. and that she didn't do any housework. Of course, she wasn't hired to do housework, and my mother encouraged her to watch Telemundo. In fact, she told Sonia she watched it all the time herself because she wanted to improve her Spanish. She had praised the ethnic dishes so highly Sonia thought she was really enjoying them.

Communication through Marguerite began. Attempts to reconcile Shirley's expectations and Sonia's understanding of her role proved futile. Shirley became angrier and more frustrated. Sonia got upset and insulted. They'd flare up at each other and then retreat to their respective corners and get on the telephone. Shirley would call me and Sonia would call Marguerite. Then, I'd call Marguerite. It went on for a few weeks and then Marguerite called one morning to say it was over. Sonia couldn't take the daily attacks and she was quitting. As nice as Sonia was, and as hard as Marguerite tried to be helpful, as much as she said "I love your mother", in the end they walked away. They knew Shirley would be *alone and unable to care for herself. Paid caregivers don't have to remain on the job providing care for difficult, unreasonable people. Family caregivers can't up and quit. Your relationship is eternal even when it isn't easy or gratifying.*

4 WHY IS FAMILY CAREGING SO DIFFICULT?

What's Different About Family Caregiving?

Time, Money, lack of Help, Role reversal, Loss of Youth, Fatigue

In our society, there is an increasing pressure to opt for in-home care when caregiving needs arise instead of choosing an institutional alternative. There are two obvious reasons why the present day bias is toward in-home care: care recipients want to remain at home in almost every instance and the financial costs to insurers, government and families is significantly lower. With the expansion of the population of people in their 70s, 80s, and 90s and even 100, the number of people requiring care is exploding. The present day cost of providing private-pay institutional care is $77,400 annually. If the rate of people entering institutional care remains constant and the price of care remains constant, as the size of the older population increases, the annual cost of institutional caregiving will increase to a figure that will wipe out personal savings, bankrupt insurers and drive government into a financial abyss. Therefore, it's not surprising that government, insurers and economists are pressing for family-based, family-provided in-home care. Caregivers and care recipients are bombarded by an information campaign that warns us of the risks of institutional care: the rate of slips and falls, infection rates, low staffing rates, elder abuse, financial exploitation, patient preferences to be at home, depression rates in institutional care, medication error rates and noncompliance rates with accreditation standards.

A family opting for institutional care over in-home care makes the choice in a defensive posture, feeling the need to explain why they are not "caring for mom", as if caring only occurs in the family home. The choice to care for another person should be just that: a choice! It should be made based on the relationship between the caregiver and the care recipient. It should be congruent with family values and culture, but also consistent with resources and constraints within each unique family. It is when these caveats are ignored and caregivers are manipulated into the caregiving role, that caregiver "burden" becomes a reality.

When Shirley was younger, 50 – 60, she spoke often of never planning to become "a burden on her family". During those years she was a caregiver for several relatives and she felt tied down and tired out by the experience. She wanted to spare us from a similar fate. On many occasions she told me she wanted to go to a nursing home when she required help with acts of daily living like those that had necessitated her becoming a caregiver for her relatives. "when I need someone to take me to the bathroom, please put me in a home!" On occasion she'd visit someone who was living in a nursing home and she'd evaluate the place as a possible future home for herself, but it was always lacking. She'd say, "When my time comes, put me in a home, but not this one." I can't recall taking her to any home, over the years that met with her approval. The other thing she said often when she was young, was that she felt people lived too long. Aging made it too difficult for the family to care for them. She said that 75 was old enough for everyone. Beyond 75, she felt there were no more contributions to make, no more goals to achieve. She was annoyed with people whose greatest accomplishment was longevity. There was a man in her senior housing complex who was 99 and counting the months until he turned 100. The resident council was planning a big bash to celebrate. All he had to do was hang in there for 12 more months. This drove Shirley mad! At each resident council meeting, they'd update the progress on the party plans: invite the mayor, notify the newspaper, invite out of town relatives, collect funds, and on and on. She felt he was wasting everyone's time. What was it he was accomplishing by staying alive? Just taking up space and time. She never wanted to be like him. Seventy-five was long enough.

She read a story about a mother and daughter who concocted a plan to help the mother to a peaceful death by suicide. She wanted to replicate that final act of caring between mother and daughter. She knew I wouldn't consider it, but she'd bring it up frequently and talk about her plans and the helpful role I could play. It was a point of contention between us.

When she was 72, my son, Daniel, was born. In one moment he became the central joy and reason for living in her life. She wanted to awaken every day to spend time with him. She gloried in his development and annoyed and bored everyone around her with her incessant bragging about him. There were so many things she wanted to do with *him and for him. Most of all she wanted to be part of his life. When she turned 73, as she blew out the candles on her cake she said she wanted to live for many more years to come. Everyone smiled and clapped when she said that, as people do at birthday celebrations, but I knew it was more than the usual birthday wish. I recognized that it was her decision not to end her life at 75. She found a reason and a purpose to live into late life and was willing to risk the ravages of aging if it came with the opportunity to be a caregiver for Daniel.*

As a young woman, caring for her own children was a burden. She was unhappy; her marriage was rocky; her finances were abysmal; her dreams of a career were crushed; she was rejected by her husband's family and felt overwhelmed by having 5 children in 6 six years. Caregiving was a burden, not a gift and she ran

*away from it. She suffered extreme
pain and sadness over the years
because of the choice she made. But
with Daniel, everything was
different. She helped raise Daniel
and watched every milestone. She
was free from the emotional pain of
failed relationships and out from
under financial pressures. She'd
accepted her disappointments and
was free to enter into a caregiving
relationship with Daniel that brought
her constant joy. She spent hours on
end sitting with him at the dining
room table playing with HotWheels.
She was never too busy or too tired.
She was there for him 100%. It was
the happiest time of her life.
Watching her, I began to realize that
it isn't the actual acts we perform as
caregivers that are burdensome, but
rather, our preparedness for the task
that makes the difference. I'd play
HotWheels for a while with Daniel
and he'd have fun. I might even*

have fun myself, for a while, but as we played I'd be thinking about preparing supper and getting the laundry folded and working on my thesis and worrying about making the mortgage payment. There was so much work to get done every day: work at home, work at the store, work at school, and then the work that's part of being a member of a family, a church, a community. Everyone has something that they need you to help with, and there just isn't enough time! How long can you sit and play HotWheels and do nothing?! But for Shirley, there wasn't anything but Daniel. There was no conflict, no divided loyalties, just caring for Daniel and being there with him.

Years later, when Daniel was a teenager and Shirley was an old woman who needed help with the activities of life, the time came to decide what the best plan was to provide for her care and safety, I recall considering her earlier testament to the appropriateness of using a nursing home as a practical solution. But I also remembered that we never visited any of her friends or family in a home that met with her approval. Conventional wisdom said I should locate a home. I had family, home, and career to consider, and I did think about it, and we talked about it. But, the 60 year old woman who thought she wanted to die by 75, and who wanted to be placed in a home rather than burden her family, was not to be found. She'd been replaced by an 85 year old who knew she'd made meaningful contributions in life, well past 75. Her help, support, advice- even when unwanted- were tremendously important. She had the occasion to bail out each of her children when we were in personal tight spots well after 75. She had a relationship with Daniel that was essential to his development. Even though she now needed help with everything she did, she felt she had more to give and there was so much more she wanted to see. She wanted to be there to encourage Daniel to keep up his efforts to complete school and graduate. Her early concept of being useless and burdensome when requiring assistance with daily life was gone. She wanted to remain in the household, watch Daniel graduate, supervise the dog and cat when we were out of the house and mostly, talk with me. There were always, so many things she wanted to tell me. I didn't always want to hear them and I didn't always agree, but she felt the need to tell me everything. There was no way we could maintain this daily dialogue if she was in a home. It was our daily interaction, in the course of living our lives that sparked the conversations. It wouldn't have happened in structured visits in a nursing home. And so, despite the advice of many wise and well-intentioned people, we made the decision to keep Shirley home until the end. It was a choice and it came with sacrifice and hard work. But it wasn't a burden. That decision initiated a phase of my life when I had the opportunity to learn a lot about myself and my values and to challenge myself to be more than I thought I could be.

There are some similarities in this regard between family caregiving and paid caregiving. Not every paid caregiver is working at his or her dream job. Not everyone fantasized about emptying bed pans, debriding bed sores, or spending

evenings with someone whose
communication skills are gone. Many
paid caregivers are low wage earners
who need to work more than one job to
support a family and are often very
tired. These factors can combine to
create caregiver burden in the paid
caregiver staff. The paid caregiver
hasn't freely chosen the professional
role he or she fills. Rather, it's been
chosen for him/her by the personal
financial needs of family; economic
factors of society, personal strengths
and weaknesses and availability of
alternate opportunities.

Time

Although there are many similarities,
there are significant differences. Paid
caregivers work in shifts. No matter
how difficult a care recipient may be to
care for, the paid caregiver knows that

in 8,7,6,5,... hours the shift will end.
The paid caregiver knows that although
the job of caregiving may go on for
years, the need to provide care to this
particular person is time-limited and
could be changed tomorrow through
reassignment, if the caregiving becomes
too stressful. The paid caregiver knows
that in 5,4,3,2,1, day(s) there'll be relief
from caregiving. The paid caregiver
knows that in time vacation will provide
relief from caregiver responsibility.

The family caregiver doesn't have the
same timeline. The responsibility for
care is 24/7. The hands-on care is
different in each situation but the tasks
don't end, and the need for care doesn't
end as long as the care recipient lives.
Even when family caregivers transition
to institutional care, the felt

responsibility for tasks formerly provided by the family caregiver remains. It is very common to see family caregivers at nursing homes on a daily basis at mealtime to make certain their loved ones are fed, because this was a task for which they were formerly responsible and they remain responsible for ensuring that it's done, and done the way that the care recipients like it. The attempt to satisfy the preferences of the care recipient continues in the transition to paid caregiving even when serious doubt exists about the care recipient's level of awareness about the care given. How common it is to hear a daughter say "Mom will be happy today, pasta's on the menu" and when you see the meal tray, it looks like a pureed pink slushy, not pasta and tomato sauce. It bears no resemblance to the taste, texture or quality of food "mom loves".

Money

What motivates someone to do
something for someone else? We live in
a commercial, capitalist economy that is
based on supply and demand. I have a
supply of something, you have a need
for it, we can make a deal for you to get
what you need and I can get what I
want. You may want more than one
thing in return for the thing I need. An
exchange may have multiple elements to
it, but always there's a cost involved in
every exchange.

Long before we used monetary systems
to govern exchanges, we bartered for
goods and services. I had something
you needed, or could do something you
couldn't do yourself and you had

something I wanted, or could do something I didn't want to do for myself, so we'd make a trade. With the advent of money, the need to trade diminished. My time, talent and treasures didn't need to be sacrificed to get my needs and wants gratified. I could give you my money. As long as I had a sufficient quantity of money I could have all that I needed. But, not everyone has a sufficient quantity of money to get needs met. How then are the needs of those individuals satisfied? Family and friends.

When it comes to caregiving needs, does it matter if care is provided by family or paid caregivers? There are some who would argue that it matters a great deal. I think they're the same crowd who argue on behalf of cloth diapers for new babies even in the face of scientific research that shows disposable diapers are associated with fewer skin rashes, less bacteria, easier work load for mom and dad and less household germs and odors. If they can no longer make the case that the diaper is superior to the disposable, they'll refocus the argument on the benefits to the environment. While that argument may be valid, it needs to be weighed against the stress on full-time working moms who need to maintain those stinky cloth diapers and the delicate bottoms of their babies. Just as in the case of the disposable diaper having benefits and liabilities, so too, paid caregiving has an upside and potential downsides. The caregivers and care recipients need to evaluate their own, unique situations to determine whether the addition of paid caregivers will be an enhancement or a detriment.

Family caregiving need not be an all or nothing arrangement. Depending upon the resources of a family, paid caregivers can be incorporated into the family caregiving plan. Paid caregivers can reduce the stress level of family caregivers by providing respite. We know that when that when caregivers have regular respite they can maintain their chosen caregiver roles and avoid feeling caregiver burden.

Although there are many benefits associated with the use of paid care givers, there are also risks. Why? The caregiver-care recipient relationship in this situation is based on money alone. Unlike family caregiving that can have many, often reciprocal elements in the relationships between relative care providers and recipients, the paid care givers relationship is based entirely on an economic exchange of money for goals and services. In most instances the care provider is an employee of a company who hires out the care giving services. Therefore, there isn't even the possibility of secondary benefits that the owner of the company might receive by going the "extra mile" *i.e.*, providing extra services for the same money as a means to enhance the business relationship. There cannot, and should not be an expectation that a paid caregiver will work additional hours, outside the scheduled shift, or will perform additional duties. How often we hear families complain that the nursing assistant who is in the home one day a week to bathe and shampoo a parent, doesn't wash the dishes or vacuum. The desire is that the paid caregiver will function the way the daughter would if she was in the family home that day. We would never expect that the cable TV guy would wash the laundry of a loved one when he is at the house to reset the cable, or that the plumber would empty the trash, but we have difficulty accepting the fact that the paid caregiver relationship is based on a formal, financial agreement to provide specific services.

How different this is from the family caregiver "contract" that is based on a lifetime of relationships, values, expectations, and experiences which may cause the care recipient to feel entitled to ask for anything and the caregiver feeling obligated to do everything asked.

I remember my mother in the last few years before she died. She needed help with almost all her activities of daily living. Various people suggested to her that she become active with a homecare program but she proudly asserted: "I don't need any help from outsiders. I have my daughter and she'll do everything!"

Sound familiar? I hear from caregivers all the time that their relatives refuse to accept outsiders into their home. Therefore, the family caregiver feels trapped into providing all the care needed. The nature of the relationship is such that the caregiver is seeking something in exchange for the services provided and it has nothing to do with money. There are probably as many reasons why caregivers hang in and provide care, no matter how difficult it becomes, as there are caregivers, because the decision to provide care is based on family relationships and there are no two relationships that are identical. One woman has a different relationship with each of her children, spouse and siblings. As a result, the caregiving relationships she has will also be different.

Within the same family, one family member may find mom to be cooperative, non-demanding and eternally grateful for any caregiving provided (This is most often the experience of the last born son.) On the other hand, the daughter who provides the bulk of care experiences mom as demanding, unreasonable and not at all appreciative. Why is mom different in each relationship? What are the expectations of each caregiver? Those factors are so complex and based on a lifelong history between each actor there is no simple answer. However, what is quickly apparent is the difference in the relationship between the family caregivers and care recipient and that of paid relationships.

Even when the family recipient pays the family caregiver, which happens in some cases, it's different from hiring professional caregivers. For some families, a relative is selected as the primary caregiver. (S)he will usually live in the care recipient's home; often give up paid employment; live and eat for free; and receive a small "payment" for services rendered. The amount paid almost never equals the cost of 24/7 in-home paid, professional care, but it is seen by the family and care recipient as "fair" value for services rendered. It rarely ends with the caregiver feeling there was equity. The requirements of family caregiving usually exceed the reimbursement provided. Family caregiving requires so much more than the services itemized in a contract.

When you are identified as the primary caregiver a mantle of responsibility is placed on your shoulders. You become responsible for the health and happiness of the person for whom you're providing care. You have to help make decisions about medical issues, end of life care, finances, lifestyle alterations. You are responsible for providing a stimulating environment, making sure social isolation doesn't become an issue, keeping the brain nimble, keeping the extended family connected. You become responsible for entertaining the family and friends who maintain contact with the care recipient and often become the "nudge" who tries to reel in absent relatives who forget to pay a visit. Holidays still need to be celebrated and the care recipient usually wants to keep up past traditions—even when they cannot. That's when the family caregiver steps in. I remember speaking with a woman who cared for her mother for 5 years. She moved home to care for her terminally ill dad, but when dad died, the family realized mom couldn't stay home alone. So, she was pressed into service "for a little while". Five years later she was still there. The tiny "pay" she received from her siblings could only support a meager life style. She was missing key years in the labor force, had no savings left, couldn't afford a car and time was quickly slipping by. It wasn't the financial drain that pushed her to give up the primary caregiver role however, it was all the Christmas preparation that came with the job!

Mom loved Christmas and always entertained and shopped for special gifts for all her children and grandchildren. Part of the unspecified role of the primary caregiver was to support that part of mom's life. So, on top of providing support for all the activities of daily living, the caregiver had to host the Christmas celebration, cook and prepare for 25 people and shop and wrap a special gift for each one. Mom paid for all of it and even said "Make sure you buy a present for yourself.", but that money could never compensate the caregiver for the amount of work it took for her to make mom feel she was still matriarch of the family. After 5 Christmases, the caregiver had had enough! There was no gift special enough to compensate her for the time, energy, loss of personal life and feeling of being sacrificed.

In addition to the physical and emotional strain on the caregiver there are also real, financial consequences to caregiving. Most employed caregivers report having to cut their work hours to accommodate caregiving needs. Many leave the workforce for a time when care needs ramp up. For many caregivers the timing couldn't be worse. People leaving the workforce at 50 something are significantly less likely to be fully employed when their caregiving duties end and they attempt to return to the workforce. Although, when they reduce, or stop employment, they also reduce or stop contributions to Social Security and pension plans at a time in life when they will not be able to make up the loss. Studies estimate that the average lifetime loss in retirement benefits experienced by caregivers due to reduced work hours is $50,000 in private pensions and $137,980 in Social Security benefits. Caregiving can have a negative, lifelong impact on the level of poverty of caregivers, particularly female caregivers.

Lack of Help

Who Takes Care of the Caregiver when the Caregiver's Busy Taking Care?

Short Answer: No One!

How many caregivers does it take to care for one mother? It doesn't matter. There's only one who'll do it anyway.

When people reminisce about the "good old days" when family cared for their own, at home, one fact they constantly fail to address is family size. Large families with 8, 10, 13 children were not uncommon. There were many people living at home to share the caring. Today, the caregiver is likely to have only 2 siblings with whom to share the care and if one of those is a brother, there is only a 35% chance that she'll get help from him. Based on population projections, going forward, the number

of potential caregiving children in a
family will shrink to 1.5 per family.

Medicare will pay for many in-home,
long term care services, as long as they
meet the criteria of "skilled" services,
but most of the care provided at home
is chronic, custodial care. Although it
may require the caregiver to develop a
new set of skills, those skills don't rise
to the Medicare level. Family members
often remark that they feel they've
learned to become nurses in the course
of caring for their loved one. Nothing
in day to day life, or liberal arts
education, teaches you how to support
the weight of your dad as you guide him
down a narrow hallway toward the
bathroom that seems miles away as he
frets and fumes about whether he'll get
there in time to avoid urinating on the
floor. There is no training for how to
help your mother feed herself after she's

had a stroke that affected her ability to swallow. No one teaches you how to care for skin that's thin and delicate and prone to breaking down. The lessons learned are learned "on the job", without the benefit of an internship program. There's no sharing of the knowledge, no passing along the "secrets" in the way family recipes are passed down. No one else wants this job. Even when other family members help out, there are limits to what they'll do. They give the caregiver some help with the caregiver's task, but they don't embrace the task as their own and learn the lessons needed to help with all the caregiving functions.

Caregiving is difficult on many levels, but it could be easier if there was more help. There are three factors that limit caregiver help: cost of paid caregiving, availability of other family members and resistance to accept help. The average cost of in-home, paid, caregiving is $11.16 per hour (AARP, 2011). Caregiving is a 24 hour responsibility. Even when paid caregivers are utilized to ease some of the physical strain of providing care, the mental strain remains. The sense of responsibility, the need to be there in case something goes wrong, the worry and fear as each month there's a need for more help as the capabilities of the person needing care diminishes.

By augmenting family care with paid care the caregiver can get some respite. A good night's sleep can make all aspects of caregiving more bearable. Fresh eyes see new solutions to problems, but at the price of paid care, family caregivers tend to only use paid care to provide assistance with tasks they can't do themselves, or to stay with the care recipient when the family caregiver is at work. Respite care provided by paid caregivers is rarely used due to the cost. Rather it is used for caregiving services that the caregiver can't perform, often because they're busy providing other caregiving services. Respite for the caregiver should be paid for by the care recipient. It's a small investment in ensuring the ongoing availability of family caregiving. It rarely happens however. More than 25% of older, widowed, adults in our country live on their Social Security check and maybe a small pension that covers basic household costs and that number is expected to increase to 53% as baby boomers retire (SSA 2012). If the elder remains home, the money available covers the cost of maintaining the home. There isn't any money to buy respite care. If the care recipient sold the family home or used a reverse mortgage, money could be available to provide more paid, long term care, but care recipients recoil at the mention of giving up their homes and families usually resist in the same way. Although, in most cases there is only one family caregiver, there are usually several "heirs" with strongly held opinions about the use of family assets. Spending their potential share of the family home on respite care for their sister isn't a decision made easily.

If respite for the caregiver is difficult to arrange due to the cost, it's nearly impossible to arrange by relying on other family members to help out. The decision to become the primary caregiver for a relative isn't usually a rational, studied decision. It happens slowly, over time. There's a gradual acceptance of more responsibility. It's rare that someone is officially appointed caregiver. In most families, it happens almost by chance. One day, you look at your situation and realize: "It's all on me." You know it, your loved one knows it and the rest of the family knows it. Their responsibilities are over. They may have worries and they may have opinions, but they don't have responsibility. That's on you. When they help out, if they do, they're doing you a "favor". They're not accepting responsibility for the caregiving needs of their parent, they're doing you a favor, when and if they have free time!

Sometimes the favors done can provide meaningful relief to an over-tired caregiver. Perhaps a sister takes mom for a week so the caregiver can have a vacation with her husband and kids. But that kind of help isn't common. What's more common is the "visit".

The other siblings of the caregiver or extended family members come by for a scheduled visit. Does this provide respite for the caregiver? It should, if the caregiver left when they arrived and took a nap. But, what usually happens is the care recipient puts pressure on the caregiver to help turn the visit into a social event. This involves ensuring there's food to serve and actually waiting on the relatives when they arrive. Instead of respite for the caregiver, the visit most often turns into added burden for the caregiver. The rest of the family has killed two birds with one stone. They've visited mom, or dad, and they've "helped" the caregiver.

In the last couple of years of my mother's life, the only time she received visitors was Mothers' Day and the Christmas/birthday visit.

Mothers' Day was always tough. Shirley wanted all her children to visit her on that day to make her feel special and forgiven for not being a great mother in the early years of our lives. Although each of her children said they forgave the past, and often acted as if they did, she felt resentment lingered. Honoring her on Mothers' Day was one way she felt affirmed that she really was forgiven. To ensure she'd be remembered on Mothers' Day she'd engineer social events to bring us all together. When she was able, she'd plan a Mothers' Day brunch at a restaurant, invite everyone, kids, grandkids and she'd pay for it all. Then she's have photos taken to review during the year showing her children all gathered to honor her.

She loved being with us all together and she loved feeling we were honoring her. In her down moments, however, she'd say to me that she "knew they wouldn't have come if she didn't pick up the tab." She's always try to find places to eat that we were eager to try, or family favorites that we couldn't afford. Always trying to ensure we'd all show up on Mothers' Day.

When it became impossible for her to plan the event and eventually even to get out to a restaurant, we switched to in-home celebrations. The planning, shopping, cooking and preparation fell to me. I never did as good a job as any of the restaurants had done. Once we tried using a caterer but my brother didn't like the food. So, although mom said she didn't think it was quite right that I, also a mother, had to spend Mothers' Day waiting on people, she insisted I plan the party and cook food that would please my brothers.

At the same time, the family structure was changing. The

grandkids were growing into adults who wanted to honor their own mothers and those mothers, including me wanted to be the center of their attention. They were willing to stop by and drop off a gift before they went off to their own Mothers' Day celebrations, but no one wanted to dedicate the day to sitting in mom's apartment and honoring her. In addition, it became increasingly difficult for her to follow all the conversations that would be happening simultaneously when 25 people were all talking to each other. They were talking and laughing about things she wasn't any part of.

Her birthday was the day after Christmas and she required that it be a day of special celebration. She wouldn't accept birthday gifts offered on Christmas day. If you wanted to give her a gift, you had to make a special visit to her on the following day. Just like Mothers'

Day, the planning for that day fell to me when she was no longer able to entertain. Like Mothers' Day it became more of a disappointment in her later years when fewer people came by to sing Happy Birthday. In her last year she remained in her bedroom on both holidays and received visitors in her bedroom. It was partly an acknowledgement that she didn't have the strength to sit at the table, but it was primarily a way to get one-on-one attention from the family.

Everyone in the family is busy. They all have more responsibilities than they can meet on a daily basis. We are a very busy, active society. Even our children are booked and scheduled into more activities than they can begin to enjoy. There's a perpetual sense of never being done with the tasks of the day. It doesn't enter into the daily life of families that someone ought to be providing respite to a caregiver; that someone should assume responsibility for a relative. If the caregiver doesn't ask for help, specify the help needed, and insist on relief, it won't be forthcoming.

And that brings up the third reason why family caregivers are so different from paid caregivers. Relief of paid caregivers is built into the job. Relief arrives at the end of the shift. Occasionally, due to staffing issues the paid caregiver is called on to work overtime, or pull a double shift, but then, there's immediate financial benefits for the extra work. Even with payment of additional money, there are limits placed on how much overtime a paid caregiver can be called on to provide. No such limits are placed on the family caregiver, not by law or statute, not by extended family members and least of all by the caregiver herself.

What's the reason family caregivers over extend themselves on a continual basis? It relates to the reason one particular person is selected as the primary caregiver. There is a relationship between the caregiver and care recipient that pulls the caregiver into the situation and keeps them there over time. It's common for caregivers to say "I had no choice. There wasn't anyone else to do it." But that isn't accurate. Perhaps there isn't anyone who would provide the care in the way and place that the care recipient wants it, but someone, somewhere will provide care if the family caregiver walks away. No one is irreplaceable. What is there in the relationship between the caregiver and care recipient that keeps the caregiver there?

In the last couple of years of my mother's life her care needs expanded. There were many occasions when I questioned myself about why I was hanging in there and continuing such a difficult job. I think there were multiple reasons and not all of them sensible, practical or carefully selected. Like many of the emotionally significant experiences in our lives, heart overruled head. Added to that is the fact that often deep-seated psychological issues that remain with us from childhood impact decisions and actions many years later in our adult lives.

When I was young there was a T.V. character, Geraldine, played by

Flip Wilson, who always blamed his questionable behavior on the devil: "The Devil made me do it!" We understand what he meant because we all wrestle with our own demons which sometimes make us do inexplicable things. So, what were the practical, sensible reasons, the emotional connections and the psychological demons that kept me serving as a caregiver for my mother?

Shirley wanted to be in her apartment, sleeping directly over our heads. She felt safe there. Moving her elsewhere would have touched off a major project. We'd have had to find a new place for her. That would mean finding a place we could accept without feeling guilty about the quality, and more difficult, convincing Shirley to give it a try. Remember, she never saw a home she approved.

My mother was the most stubborn person I've ever known. She would *dig in her heels on an issue and maintain her position, irrespective of the facts or consequences. Appeals to logic never dissuaded her when she didn't want to do something. Even if we found a place and she agreed to go, there was so much to do to make it happen. She was not a woman of financial means. She lived on her Social Security check and pension. There were no assets to liquidate to pay for care. On the one hand, that meant she'd be eligible for Medicaid, but on the other, it meant going through the application process. One of the sticking points was her life insurance policy. Shirley pre-planned her funeral down to the smallest detail. She priced out the cost with the funeral director and purchased life insurance policies to cover the projected cost. She made many sacrifices to pay for the insurance policies. Because she purchased them late in life, the* premiums were high. To pay the price she stopped having the hair dresser come to the house to do her hair and she gave up the expense of maintaining platinum blonde hair. She told everyone she felt it was time to go gray, but it was just the cost that caused her to change her look. She stopped her frequent catalog shopping and cancelled home delivery of the newspaper. This insurance was very important to her.

Unfortunately, it was also important to Medicaid who views insurance as an asset to be liquidated or consigned to the State before qualifying for benefits. Only a portion of the insurance benefit could be used for funeral costs but Shirley had planned a funeral that required all the money. And she was too stubborn to change her plan. She wouldn't even discuss it. Without Medicaid money, there wasn't enough money to pay for care in another setting. *Taking on the battle over the insurance policies seemed more difficult at the end of the work day than just continuing to provide care at home.*

On an emotional level, I loved her and I didn't want her to end her life in a nursing home. For most of my life she was the best mother she knew how to be to me. She made many sacrifices for me throughout the years and I wanted to take care of her.

And then, there are the demons. Shirley abandoned me when I was a child. Although she came back when I was a young adult and spent the remainder of her life trying to compensate for the missing years, the scars from abandonment don't go away. I didn't want to repeat her pattern. I didn't want to abandon her when the caregiving got tough. I needed to prove to myself that I wasn't that type of person. Commitment and loyalty have deep meaning for me and I had to live that in my life with her. I also wanted my son to see and experience that in our family we don't dispense with loved ones just because caring for them is difficult. I felt it was important for my son to witness commitment and recognize that in our family we are bonded through love and commitment and not convenience.

The dynamics of family relationships are complex, classic and predictable when analyzed as a collection of "types", but they are unique and unpredictable within each family. Family relationships are based on love and not financial incentives, there can be many rewards the caregiver is seeking in return for the care provided. Perhaps the caregiver is seeking approval from a parent or acknowledgement as an adult, no longer a kid who screws things up. Perhaps the caregiver is trying to compensate for disappointing the parent with their choices and decisions at an earlier age and gain forgiveness. Some caregivers are trying to demonstrate their competence, maybe their superiority over a sibling. Sometimes the caregiver is driven by a desire to do the "right thing". They have a standard about what's right regarding treatment of family and they are determined to live up to their standard. Sometimes they have no personal standard but are aware of a family-held standard and they want to live up to the standards of others, to demonstrate they're doing the right thing.

Whether it's love, guilt, pride or shame that drives the caregiver is irrelevant. In the end, what matters is that they've made the choice to do what's necessary to enable another to live life as he or she wanted. Whatever the underlying, perhaps unconscious motivation, the act should be applauded.

For several years I've had the opportunity to participate in the Fearless Caregiver Conference. The conference is organized by a national media group, who have successfully utilized the Internet and print media to provide information and support to family caregivers. Each year, throughout the country they stage conferences to bring caregivers together to help them recognize the powerful work they do as caregivers and applaud the caregiver's commitment to family. Hundreds of men and women attend each conference and the reaction of caregivers to the experience is moving. Validating, applauding, recognizing sacrifice, cheering small successes, are actions that cause caregivers to smile. One after the other, caregivers tell me how important it was to them to hear people acknowledge and applaud the personal sacrifices they've made on behalf of a family member.

There are many important issues our society can and should address regarding family caregiving, such as providing pay for caregivers, adjusting Social Security calculations, expanding respite options, to name a few. However, these are not the issues attendees at the conference talk about. Rather, it is the appreciation by others of the work it takes to be a caregiver and applause for sacrifices they have willingly made. Even if social policy takes many more decades to catch up with the needs of society, we can improve the quality of life for today's caregivers by applauding their efforts, acknowledging their expertise and thanking them for their commitment.

What makes it so difficult for the caregiver to ask for help? Is it that the act of asking, even if the request isn't honored, diminishes the sought after, impact of caregiving.

If I provide care out of a feeling of pure love and want that love returned to me by the care recipient, I run the risk of getting less love if I share the task of giving care with someone else. Perhaps the care recipient will love the person I called in to help more than me , and she'll get more love from the care recipient than I will. If I've had an issue with feeling unloved in the past, the chance that I'll feel less loved by sharing the caregiver task is great.

If I am compensating for a turbulent youth by being a dedicated caregiver, will I free myself from guilt if I am asking for help with the care? Probably not. Working out guilt usually involves feeling the need to sacrifice. If you help me with my tasks, I still feel guilty for my past and now, I also feel guilty for placing a burden on you. Guilt begets guilt. It doesn't get worked off like a debt to be repaid. Caregivers limit guilt by not asking for help.

Caregivers who are trying to live up to self- imposed standards continually move the bar so that no matter how hard they work, they never reach a sense of fulfillment because they always could have done more. If they call in the troops for help, they're failing to meet their standard and although the tasks of caregiving are accomplished, the underlying purpose of caregiving hasn't been achieved.

Shirley was a caregiver many times throughout her life. In the early years she was appointed caregiver by her parents and with that assignment came lifelong feelings of resentment. In later years she became a caregiver because she believed there was no one else who would provide care for her sisters. She felt angry and self-righteous about the caregiving role. In both situations it was impossible to see how caregiving could be a gift. But when she became a caregiver for her aunt Stella, she had the opportunity to see how caregiving can provide the chance to work through relationships and alleviate guilt.

Aunt Stella was Shirley's mother's sister. When Shirley's mother was sick and dying, Shirley wasn't there. She'd abandoned her family and didn't even know her mother needed her. The guilt about that choice haunted Shirley for life and was the driving force in many of the decisions she made in late life. When Stella needed full time care, Shirley stepped forward and committed herself to the task. Every day she took the bus across town to Aunt Stella's tiny efficiency apartment and helped her bathe, made breakfast, tidied her small apartment and talked with her. Aunt Stella knew she didn't have a lot of time left and she wanted to tell every story she knew; all the important things in life that she'd learned. She wanted to talk to someone who would listen and value the history of the family. Shirley was the perfect person for the task. She bought a tape recorder and recorded those conversations and transcribed them each evening so Stella could witness the legacy of her life that she was creating.

They'd stop each day to watch Family Feud and Match Game on T.V. and then Shirley would prepare something for dinner. They'd eat together and then Shirley would clean up and help Stella prepare for bed. Once she was settled, Shirley would catch the bus and travel back across town. On weekends, she'd stop in town and buy groceries and *carry them, on the bus, to Stella's apartment. Although there weren't a lot of bags, because they didn't need much food, it was still difficult for Shirley to manage on the bus. But she never asked for help. She was providing care to her aunt because she hadn't been there for her mother. Her aunt was sharing stories about the family, many about Shirley's mother and it helped Shirley feel reconnected to her family. Aunt Stella praised and thanked her often, and wisely, said things like "Lee would be so proud of the way you're helping me. She helped everyone in the family." (Lee was Shirley's mother).*

Shirley desperately wanted to believe this was true. She wanted absolution for her sins. If she couldn't receive it directly from her mother, then getting it from her mother's sister, who knew her so well, was the next best thing. Shirley didn't ask for help caring for Aunt Stella, and she didn't ever tell many people in the family that she was doing it. The chores were difficult and the responsibility was great but the reward of feeling closer to her family and forgiven by her mother, was tremendous.

One of the greatest sources of pride and feeling of accomplishment was that she was able to keep Aunt Stella at home, avoiding nursing home care, as Stella wanted. These feelings were a gift to a woman who was filled with guilt and regret throughout much of her life. As a result of her caregiving sacrifices she was able to begin seeing herself as a whole person, not simply defined by

> *the mistakes she made. Rather, she was a mosaic of mistakes, failed attempts and incredible sacrifices for others and successes.*

Paid caregivers openly seek all the help they can get with caregiving tasks. Their focus is on the task. They aren't trying to work out long term relationship issues. Although it's rarely acknowledged, family caregiving and the sacrifices it entails provides a unique opportunity to resolve issues, deepen relationships and develop into the person you seek to become. Herein lays the gift of caregiving.

Guilt, feelings of inadequacy, and unrealistic personal standards are issues, that arise often in caregiver relationships. Unfortunately, they can also result in caregiving that degenerates into angry, conflicted relationships. When we are involved in completing a task that's challenging, we're well advised to seek out help. We need information and training to enhance our skills, help with tasks and support to ensure success. This is especially true for caregivers.

Caregivers who participate in support groups are less likely to perceive caregiving as a burden and less likely to become burned out. Feelings of anger, guilt and inadequacy are heavy burdens to carry. With the weight of these feelings strapped to your back, it's very difficult to stand tall and also carry the weight of your loved one, who needs you.

Support can come in many forms but it usually includes having someone to talk with about what you're thinking and feeling. For many people, a close friend can provide the support needed, for many, many others support is best provided by someone in the same situation, through support groups. For some, a therapist is a wise choice. If you've carried deeply rooted feelings, for years, and now as a caregiver they're creeping into your daily life, this might be the perfect time to address old issues and move forward. The opportunity of caregiving can be a powerful impetus for personal growth.

Role Reversal

In all relationships there is a power dynamic. At any point in time, one person has more power than the other.

In positive relationships the power shifts from one to the other depending upon the situation. When one person has more knowledge, skill, experience or talent in a given area, that person has the power. This is the nature of healthy relationships. In adult/child relationships the power dynamic resides with the adult who is usually bigger, stronger, wiser and possess the resources in the relationship. Eventually, the child grows up and the adult/child relationship matures into a satisfying adult/adult relationship. Naturally, there are relationships which evolve less smoothly than others, but the goal is a mature adult/adult relationship with power shared and decisions made by both parties.

We become comfortable within these roles and then the need for caregiving arises and the relationship changes. When one person is dependent upon another to complete common tasks of daily living, the power in the relationship shifts away from the care recipient and to the caregiver. As the care recipient's need for care increases and expands to additional areas of life, the dependence on the caregiver increases and the power in the relationship is further shifted in favor of the caregiver. Although most caregivers would readily cede the power back to the care recipient if that person had the capacity to resume independent functioning, the reality is that by the time a caregiver has assumed power within the relationship, there is small chance that the care recipient will ever resume independent functioning.

This shift in power signals a reversal of roles when the caregiving relationship is between parent and child. In the early years of the relationship the parent had all the power. As the child developed the relationship matured and the power was shared by parent and child. Now, in the caregiving relationship, the power lies with the adult child who is providing care.

The power shift results in a reversal in the roles of parent and child. The child becomes the decision maker, the provider of protection, the one with the responsibility of meeting basic needs for the parent. There's been much discussion of the impact this has on the parent and there is caregiver "advice" in abundance, that exhorts caregivers to respect the dignity of the parent, to avoid diminishing the apparent power of the parent when providing care. In reality, however, despite the caregiver's best intentions to maintain an equal, adult/adult relationship, the needs and limitations of the care recipient eventually results in the caregiver assuming responsibility for the decisions made within the relationship.

This phenomenon occurs irrespective of the talent, skills, experience or knowledge of the caregiver. In a manner similar to the parent/child power dynamic, when the parent has the power, even when their capacity to perform the duties of the role are limited, caregivers have the power over the care recipients. I recall meeting a caregiver at a community forum. She was a distracted, disheveled 50 ish woman who had questions about the availability of in-home services for her mother. She described a situation in which her mother lived with her in the family home. Mom needed assistance with most activities but could feed herself and walk independently within the home, but did not recognize where she was walking, or remember why she stood up to walk. For a couple of years the daughter was providing care for mom and "running the house". Several community agencies were involved in helping to provide care but none remained because the house was extremely cluttered and agencies diagnosed the daughter as a hoarder. Elderly Protective Services was involved with the family, trying to protect the mother and simultaneously honor her expressed wish to remain at home. The staff of the agencies reported that the daughter's mental health issues caused her to be incapable of adequately meeting mom's needs. Her decisional capacity was severely limited. However, she remained the decision-maker for her mother. She decided what groceries to buy and when or whether to eat. She decided whether or not to fill a prescription or take mom to the doctor. She decided whether a change in health status was an emergency requiring immediate attention or something that could wait for the next scheduled doctor's visit. Her hoarding created a home setting that caused her mom to live amid debris and disorganization. Clearly, her skills and talents were not the reason why she was the caregiver, but because of her relationship with her mom, she became the caregiver and stepped into the role reversal, and she had the power in the relationship. The responsibilities heaped on caregivers can be overwhelming. The physical and mental stresses are obvious but may be the least difficult for the caregiver to accept. So often, we see caregivers just put their heads down, put one foot in front of the other and complete the tasks before them. They do what needs to be done. They don't know how they get it done, they just do it!

But what is more difficult to accomplish, is dealing with the emotions associated with reversing roles with one's parent. Most often, this is the part of caregiving that is ignored by the caregiver and by society. As long as the work is getting done and the caregiver hasn't collapsed under the strain, we (caregiver and the rest of the world) push the emotional component down into a deep, private place to be visited only in the occasional nightmare that wakens us from sleep with the frightening feeling that we're alone and vulnerable in a big, scary world.

It's at those moments that our unconscious is reminding us that things are changing. We are no longer any one's baby. There is no strong daddy or gentle loving mommy who is watching over us, waiting, anticipating, our every cry. There is no one ready to sacrifice their time, energy, life, if need be, to protect and care for us. We'll never again be another's proudest accomplishment.

It's commonly reported that, whatever their age…or yours, when your parents die, you realize you're an orphan. It's a hard, cold reality. It doesn't matter how little of the parent was remaining prior to the death, as long as they are alive, the potential exists, (or the fantasy continues) that one day you'll fulfill the potential they saw in you, and they'll provide the love and acceptance you dreamed about.

Once they're gone, the dream is over, but before that happens, if you are a caregiver, you experience the change in your relationship that requires you to give to your parent the protection and assistance they require and the love and acceptance you seek. Recognizing that childhood has ended, permanently, is difficult for most of us. We take with us so many unfulfilled dreams and have so many tasks we failed to achieve and we fear they will never be accomplished.

I remember my father saying to me when I got my driver's license (a developmental milestone), " You realize you'll never be able to just curl up on he back seat and be taken home again?" I know he was talking about the difference between being a carefree kid and a responsible, licensed adult. That transition was so exciting and filled with potential glory, it was easy to ignore his admonition and just revel in the thoughts of my future as an independent driver. Free from parental constraints, able to travel, vacations, so much potential. But Dad was right in his warning. Driving is a big responsibility, a huge expense and filled with potential for stress and even sadness. Becoming a caregiver, switching roles with a parent is likewise a major responsibility filled with stress and strain, but if we recognize what we're doing and why we are doing it, the love and acceptance that we want and need is a part of the caregiving that provides a gift of adulthood. In caregiving we begin to realize our potential as generative beings who are truly capable of giving and receiving love.

I don't know exactly when Shirley and I began to shift roles, but by the end of the caregiver relationship, the reversal was complete. I was the one who made all the decisions: healthcare, residence, budgeting, shopping. I did it partly because the power had shifted but mostly because Shirley ceded her authority to me. As she aged and became more frail, she turned to me to protect her. If I asked her, "What would you like for dinner tonight mom?" She would reply: "What do you think would be good for me honey?" or I'd ask "Do you think you're feeing up to going to see the doctor this week?" She'd answer "If you think I need to go, I'll go." "Do you want to watch the news on CNN?" "You can turn it on if you want to watch it." There was absolutely no area in which she would express a choice. She turned every decision, no matter how small, over to me. I, of course, as every expert suggests, was trying to be a sensitive caregiver and kept creating opportunities for her to express her wishes so she could maintain some personal power in her role, but it only served to make me frustrated. It was easier for both of us to have me make the decisions, tell her what to do and move one.

She didn't seem to mind that approach, but it was painful for me. I wanted her to have some power in our relationship. I wanted her to still be mom: argumentative, opinionated, decisive, but it couldn't happen.

Loss of Youth

We begin life growing and developing, changing constantly. Becoming more. Long before we comprehend the fact that we are changing we experience the changes. Our bodies and minds are expanding along with our hearts and spirits. As we develop and our awareness of change sharpens we eagerly anticipate change: developing breasts, building bi-ceps, becoming taller, voice deepening. It's all exciting and positive. We anticipate developmental milestones associated with growth like school, career, marriage, parenthood. All the growth and development is associated with being young. It's what youth do, they grow, develop, change. We mark the accomplishments with tick marks on height charts, birthday celebrations, graduation ceremonies, weddings and birth announcements. We are building our lives and life is in front of us, seemingly limitless in opportunities and duration. For all of us there is a crossover point when there is less time before us than what has already passed. When there are fewer celebrations to mark life events, when physical changes have ceased to be a joy to behold and instead a cause for concern. Change in our youth is celebrated. Change in later life is generally resisted. Even social changes, that many eagerly await are confounded by mixed emotions because it occurs when we are old. It is the name tag that identifies us as officially "old": retired. Yesterday, you were a nurse, age unknown, obviously, from your appearance, not 21, but what age? No one knew-or cared. Today you are retired and the calculation begins. She must be at least 66 because she can't collect her full Social Security before then. Now, you're old. As a society we know retirement is a marker for old age. Some people resist and defer retirement putting off the association with aging for themselves and others. In so doing they can maintain the fantasy that they are still young. We are so reluctant to think of ourselves as old. We observe all around us that old people are ignored, their ideas and opinions disregarded, their interests and preferences in food, style, fashion, entertainment discounted. We resist becoming a member of that group.

But, for many of us the lure of retirement and the freedom it can provide is a sufficient lure to join the group and face the fact that we are now officially old. We get bumper stickers that remind us and those who drive behind us that we may be old but we're still here; we join clubs that are determined to show the world that we may be old but we still want to have fun and we may show it by wearing silly red hats. We volunteer, and often work harder, for no pay, than we worked in the last few years of our careers. We want to show the world we're still productive. We advocate for causes to show the world that we still have a voice. We weigh the tradeoffs of being old versus being retired. Most of us determine that retirement is terrific and would have been even better if only we could have retired while we were young enough to really enjoy it and then return to work when we're old and there's nothing else to do.

It is extremely difficult to get past the negative associations with aging and fully embrace being old as another opportunity for development. By the time we accept the fact that we've become old we are too exhausted to embrace development. We are trying so hard to hold back the hands of time, we have no energy for late life development. We cause ourselves to become the older person we dread: living in the past; resisting change; unable to recognize the changes in ourselves and see them as a positive association with the fulfillment of a lifetime of effort to become the person we are and a marker on the path to whom we will become when fully developed.

When we become a family caregiver for our parent, at whatever age, and we experience the role reversal that occurs, we are forced to recognize that we are no longer young. Irrespective of our age at that point, we stop being the kid and are forced to recognize, even if only at the unconscious level, that we are no longer young. Children lack the capacity to assume the responsibility for the care of a parent. Although we know there are many dysfunctional families where children are forced to assume adult responsibilities due to the failure of parents to fulfill their roles, as a society we recognize that this isn't appropriate. There is no pretense that this is a healthy development and it doesn't signal a developmental milestone. In fact, just the opposite, it is assumed that it is a a developmental block that will result in a developmental crisis which will require attention in later stages of life.

That isn't the case with the adult family caregiver. As a rule the caregiver is a fully functioning adult who has developed sufficiently biologically, psychologically and socially to assume the responsibilities of caregiving without creating developmental crises. The caregiver is able to surmount the challenges of becoming a caregiver, but not without difficulty. Once the caregiver realizes and ultimately accepts the fact of becoming a caregiver and acknowledges the role reversal that has taken place, there is a corollary acknowledgement that recognizes "I am no longer young."

The concept of carefree youth, although rarely recognized and appreciated as we pass through that stage of life, is lost for ever. When the work of a caregiver is finally over, the caregiver doesn't revert to carefree youth. At best, one is wiser, more compassionate, more developed emotionally and spiritually, ...and older. Youth, and the dreams which were slipping away for years are now gone for good. Hopefully, they're replaced with more meaningful, attainable dreams for the next step in life. Sometimes they're replaced with sadness and anger about all the that might have been. Life after caregiving provides us with choices about the next phase of life, but first there has to be an acceptance of the stage of life we are actually in, and a willingness to release the notions of the past.

When I turned 50, a wise friend told me the secret to happiness after 50 is to "lower your standards." I was appalled. What was the implication? Because I was 50 I couldn't do things the way I used to? I knew I could so anything I wanted or needed to do, and my life after 50 has proven that to me. But, she was right, nonetheless. I realized that if I held the same standards for myself as I had in decades previous, I was consigning myself to plans and actions that were designed when I was much younger. My values were being formed. My priorities and therefore my standards of performance were based on issues that had little or no relevance or importance in my life at fifty. I didn't have to continue doing everything I had done previously, and in the way, and to the extent I had done it before. By releasing myself from those standards I had time, energy, imagination and resources to do new things; enjoy things I hadn't dreamed of before and to accomplish new things I had never dreamed of previously.

Shirley never accepted her aging. She never imagined her future or set goals for life as a fully functioning adult. Shirley retained childlike expectations of life and love. Despite ample evidence to the contrary, she maintained the fantasy that her mother and father had a perfect marriage. She insisted her father was a perfect husband who anticipated her mother's every need and spent his days and nights thinking of ways to please her. She remembered her mother as a domestic goddess who lived to please her family. Cooking and cleaning was all Mama wanted to do in life and she was perfect at both according to Shirley.

In fact, her mother wrestled with chronic depression and alcoholism. Her father spent sad, lonely nights trying to convince her to go to bed to "sleep it off". Her father sought a happier life by being away from the family home as much as possible. He was involved in local politics and community theater. He helped his brother in law, Bill, put on musical variety shows in which Shirley often performed, along with her sisters. She and her father loved these shows and the attention it brought them. Her mother resented them. She did everything she could to delay their departure each evening as they went off to rehearsals. According to other relatives, her mother and father argued frequently because Shirley and her dad went out each night and left Mama home alone. Her father used to say "Don't be jealous Lee. I'm not doing anything wrong. I'm with my best girls." The "best girls" loved the attention they got, Lee, not so much.

They had a marriage similar to many others from that era. Not a lot of communication about feelings.

No role for women outside the family home. Recognition of women based on their domestic talents, beauty and performance abilities. Hardly Utopian. But, Shirley never allowed herself to see her parents as people with real feelings, challenges and life experiences. People to be admired for all they actually achieved instead of a fantasy from childhood wishes.

Because Shirley failed to accept reality, she based her life on a fantasy. She continuously looked for "perfect" men who would anticipate her every need and make her perfectly happy-just like her mother. . She totally missed the point that her mother wasn't happy and her marriage wasn't perfect. She failed to appreciate how hard her parents worked to keep their marriage together despite the depression and the drinking and the jealousy. She denied the stress and challenges her parents faced and preferred a romanticized version of their lives. Therefore, she failed to take away any lessons learned from their lives.

She entered the "old" stage of her life filled with a sense of personal failure for not having had a perfect marriage or perfect life.

Part of the perfect life included having perfect children who cared for her, joyfully, without complaint, no matter what she demanded. That was another disappointment she was destined to experience. None of her children provided joyful caregiving. Most of them provided no caregiving at all. I did my best to be a good caregiver, but I never even dreamed about being a joyful caregiver. I was, after-all, making a sacrifice and felt there was little to be joyful about in that situation.

Caregiving, in the years toward the end of Shirley's life gave me the opportunity to understand her.

When I was young, we just argued about things we disagreed on. But when I was older, and spending so much time with her, I began to really listen and understand why she was so unreasonable. Why she was impossible to please. She expected perfection and I wasn't perfect.

Once I understood that I couldn't ever please her, I stopped trying. I didn't stop caring for her, I just stopped trying to do it perfectly. I learned to accept doing the best I could in a given situation. It was one of the most liberating experiences in life. I began to see that in so many ways I was like Shirley. I was setting standards and goals for myself based on faulty memories from childhood. It affected my parenting, my relationship with my husband, my work, even my faith life. Once I could let go of ideas fixed in my mind in childhood and began to

> *reevaluate each aspect of my life based on who I am as an adult, life got much better and freer. Without the gift of caregiving I would not have that freedom as I enter my own "old" age.*

Recognizing that you are no longer young is not a bad thing. It is a herald to embrace the future.

Fatigue

Herbert Benson, Harvard University, defined stress as "any situation that requires behavioral adjustment. Any change to which you have to adjust is stressful." Simply stated, stress is fatigue. That which makes us tired stresses us. Some people will argue that there is good stress and bad stress. They're wrong. They assert that if you enjoy what you're doing it isn't stressful. It is

extremely important to separate yourself
from this notion. If the activity in
which you are engaged has tired you
out, you're in a state of stress and
vulnerable to all the risks associated
with stress, physical, emotional and
social.

When it comes to caregiving, there's a
"blame the victim" mentality that
implies that if the caregiver is feeling
stressed, it's because they don't really
like being a caregiver. It's their attitude
about caregiving that's the problem.
This is an over-simplification of the
stress. We have research studies that
demonstrate that caregivers who care
for parents with dementia have fewer
positive things to say about caregiving
and report more stress. The conclusion
then is made, if you don't like
caregiving, it's more stressful. Well,

obviously, there's some truth to that, but why don't they enjoy caregiving as much as their counterparts caring for non-demented parents? Perhaps because it's a lot more work! Communicating with someone with dementia is very difficult. It doesn't come naturally. It often flies in the face of all we believe about communication.

Back in the 1960s when I was new to working with people with dementia, reality orientation was the recommended method of communication. I recall the nursing home where I worked had street signs made and posted them at the intersections of each hallway to remind people where they were. Clocks were everywhere, as were calendars. We spent countless hours telling patients where they were, what day it was, who they were, and why they were in the nursing home. They never remembered. We repeated the same litany multiple times each day. We hated it. We also encouraged the families to do the same. When mom called you Josephine, because she thought you were her sister, correct her. Tell her you're her daughter. Over and over. And what happens when you correct mom? She becomes upset. "Don't tell me you're my daughter! My daughter is down the hall in the nursery. What have you done with her? I want my baby! Why are you lying to me?" And the poor daughter is trying to inject "reality" "No mom, I'm your daughter. I'm grown up. Aunt Josephine died last year after daddy died. That's why you're living in the nursing home now." Maybe there's a glimmer of memory, and then tears, upset and sadness over the "news" that life is over and her loved ones are dead. Over and over, the same sad interchange. Communicating with a person with dementia can be exhausting. Who would enjoy this? Interactions like this leave the caregiver spent. It isn't about wanting to care for mom, or not wanting to care for mom. It's about the exhaustion associated with the task. It's the feeling of failure which drains the caregiver even more because she can't relieve the distress of her mom.

Fortunately, we've learned a lot about communicating with people with dementia and paid caregivers are trained to avoid those communication traps, but family caregivers don't come to the job with training certifications. They're on the job, eager and willing but rarely ready because they haven't been prepared. Performing difficult tasks for which they are not adequately trained is a source of stress for all people. Research also demonstrates that people experience extreme stress when in situations where they feel a lack of control over the outcome, lack of preparation to handle the tasks, and responsibility for the situation. That pretty much describes caregiving in the early stages. You have no control over the physical or mental changes in your parent that have necessitated your becoming a caregiver. You have no training about their illness, management of their symptoms, skills to perform the required tasks, and you regard it as one of the most important things you've ever had to do. The health, safety and life of someone you love rests on your shoulders.

On the physical side of caregiving there are many things the professionals know that make performance of a task easier. There is adaptive equipment that can make life easier, but the family caregiver only learns about them through accidental self-discovery.

You don't take training on caregiving. Pass a test. Get your license. It's like parenting. All, on the job training. As a result, everything the caregiver does is a little harder than it has to be.

I remember watching a woman trying to get her elderly mother out of the car. She was standing on the passenger side of the car with the door open telling her mother to lift her feet and pivot on the seat so she was facing the open doorway. Then she could help lift her to a standing position. Mom wasn't budging. She just kept staring at the dashboard. The daughter was increasingly frustrated and unsure about what to do next. We were able to help her get mom turned out of the car eventually. Later I told her about an inexpensive adaptive devise that she could put on mom's seat before she gets in the car. Then she doesn't need mom's "cooperation" to get out of the car. She can turn mom on the disc, assist with her legs and Presto!, she can stand. The next time I saw her she was full of thanks and praise. This little bit of information made her caregiving less stressful. Why? Not because her attitude changed, but because it was less work to get mom out of the car and therefore, less tiring.

The daily performance of difficult caregiving tasks tires the caregiver and becomes a major source of stress. Stress is easily relieved through rest.

During periods of rest the body rejuvenates itself. During sleep we are restored biologically on the cellular level, psychologically, on the emotional level and spiritually on the level of faith. After sleep we feel better. We're less tired and therefore feel able to handle the physical tasks of caregiving. We feel more relaxed and calm and we have a more positive attitude about the future. Problems that seem unsolvable at bedtime can be faced with renewed vigor in the morning…after a good nights sleep.

However, all too often, caregivers fail to have a "good night's sleep" that's so necessary to stress relief. The needs of the care recipient don't magically disappear in the evening. The need to be walked into the bathroom may arise 2 or 3 times throughout the night. Bed linens may need to be changed.

Medications may need to be administered every 4 hours. For the family caregiver who provides care on one continuous shift, there is no relief. Sleep is interrupted and the caregiver frequently feels like a thief in the night, stealing moments of rest.

The human body is strong and resilient. We can tolerate periods of hard work and inadequate sleep, but eventually it catches up with us if relief isn't provided. Even the caregiver who has no physical demands for caregiving, the physical stress on the caregiver can still be significant. If the caregiver is awake, listening for sounds of distress from another room, up at night, checking on the care recipient, watching to see the chest moving up and down indicating breathing is OK, then the caregiver isn't getting the needed restorative sleep. Over time, the effect is an accumulative build-up of physical, mental and spiritual stress.

A stressed body, attempting to perform the typical activities of the day is at great risk of injury. In states of stress, we make more mistakes. Everything we do becomes riskier. When we drive in a state of stress, we are distracted drivers. Our minds are not on the driving. We are back home worrying about the person we've left behind. "Will she be alright while I'm at the store?" "Will she try to go down to the basement and fall on the stairs?" "Will this new medication help?" So much distraction!

Fatigue isn't only mental, leading to distraction. It's also physical. When we're tired, i.e. stressed, our reflexes are slower, our reaction time is slower, we're weaker in general. Someone pulls out in front of us and we don't stop as quickly as needed…BOOM! We're in an accident.

We don't take the trouble to turn fully and look over our shoulder when we're backing up because we're tired. We just glance in the rear view mirror. Crunch! We back onto something. We're carrying the groceries up the stairs and we don't have the strength to lift out legs and we trip, OUCH! We've fallen down the steps.

We know how to drive. We know how to walk. It isn't a question of knowledge, information or training. We're just too tired to execute the tasks at hand. We are Stressed! The way to reduce stress in our lives is twofold: 1. Reduce workload and 2. Increase rest. If you've chosen to be the caregiver and, after thoughtful review of the situation you determine there is absolutely no way the workload can be reduced and still maintain the level of care you want to provide, then the only solution lies in increasing rest.

However, there is a third way to approach the problem which many, maybe most caregivers employ and it's a ticket on a train that's headed for derailment. It calls for the caregiver to maintain the work level and at times, even increase it, maintain the fatigue level, unrelieved by rest and just wait and see what happens. Allow the situation to dictate instead of taking control of the situation. This path will lead to disaster. Here is where the frightening statistics on caregiving come into play:

According to the National Alliance for Caregiving, 23% of family caregivers caring for a loved one for five or more years report their health is poor. Three quarters of family caregivers admit to not going to doctors as often as they should and 55% skipping their own medical appointments, due to caregiving demands. The Center on Aging Society reports that one in ten family caregivers claim caregiving has resulted in deteriorated health. Perhaps of greatest concern is the fact that caregivers experiencing extreme stress lose 10 years of life.

Depending on the study selected 40% - 70% of family caregivers meet diagnostic criteria for major depression. The difference in numbers is based on the type of care provided and the type of care recipient, i.e. spouse, parent, sibling, elderly, middle—aged, child, chronically ill, terminally ill, living with care giver, living apart. Family caregivers have chronic health problems including high rates of heart disease, impaired immune systems, hypertension, sleep disturbance and death.

It doesn't matter if the caregiver has a Pollyanna attitude about caregiving or is full of doom & gloom and resentment, if she is exhausted and chronically lacking respite, she will suffer the ill effects of stress. All caregivers require respite breaks and a plan for adequate sleep each day. Failure to ensure the family caregiver is receiving the rest needed will result in terrible outcomes for the caregiver and destruction of the care plan for the recipient. There will no longer be a family caregiver to provide care.

I recall talking with a woman in the emergency room where she'd taken her chronically ill dad who had another crisis episode caused by his advanced emphysema. He wasn't an easy man to care for. He spent his days fearing each breath would be his last, constantly gasping for air, despite being on continuous oxygen. He was anxious and cranky and she was the person he saw day and night, so she was the recipient of his constant complaining and angry outbursts. He required frequent suctioning to remove mucus blocks that formed in his throat. She performed this task but never felt comfortable doing it. It revolted her and she had to fight the impulse to vomit as she suctioned him. But, she did it because he needed it and when she finished and he could breathe again, he used his precious breath to criticize her about her lack of skill. Hers was a very difficult caregiving path. She looked weary and worn out as we sat in the waiting room and she said to me "The only way I'll get any relief from this is for me to die. I know he'll out live me." Many caregivers have expressed the same thought. "He'll bury me." Wives who provide chronic care to husbands with heart disease often are relieved of their caregiving duties when they have their own heart attack and the family realizes others have to pitch-in because she can't do it any longer. What a sad way to get respite.

All work demands breaks if tasks are to be performed well. A simple psychology experiment in Psych 101 demonstrates this phenomenon to college freshmen. Take a simple task, like placing a needle on a phonograph record, an easy to learn task, although one without any applicable purpose in the modern world. The first few times you try to do it, you may miss place the arm and get into the wrong groove on the record. Quickly, however, you'll get the hang of it and can consistently place the needle in the groove. If however, I ask you to continue picking up the arm and returning it to the arm rest and then placing it back in the first groove of the record, after many successful attempts, instead of getting better and better at the task, you'll begin to miss the groove. If you continue to execute the task, you'll miss by a mile. You'll find yourself taking aloud "This is silly. Why can't I put the needle in the groove? I know how to do it. It's so easy, anyone can do it." But suddenly, you can't. Not because you don't want to. Not because you have a bad attitude, just simply because fatigue has set in. Your system is experiencing a state of stress caused by the fatigue that develops when you perform the same task over and over without rest. How do we know it's just fatigue and not some mysterious affliction that prevents you from performing such a rudimentary task? Just stop and rest for a bit. Take a break from the action and then, without additional training or equipment, or emotional support from a personal trainer, pick up the arm and place the needle on the first groove. You'll get it done quicker and with greater ease than your best previous attempt. You didn't forget how to do it. You didn't decide that you didn't want to do it any longer. You just were tired from performing the same action over and over without a break.

As a rule, there isn't an emotional component to this simple psychology experiment. The fatigue is purely physical, but just imagine how much greater the strain and how much more significant the consequences of performing poorly when the task is caring for another person. Here there is always an emotional component factored into the process. This is why family caregiving is so much more stressful than paid caregiving. The paid professional caregiver has only to deal with the fatigue of the physical acts of care. They are primarily free of the emotional factors that are basic components of family life.

Unlike the psychology experiment where there is an objective, obvious standard against which you can measure the quality of your performance, caregiving lacks such a measuring stick. The impact of our actions may take time to reveal itself. We may never realize that the way we did something made things worse at times for the care recipient, the person we love and for whom we're making this "sacrifice".

Often we're too tired to observe the impact of our actions. We are just focused on all we have to do and what would happen if we failed to get it done. How rare is the moment when the caregiver stops to evaluate the quality of what he/she is doing, or examines its impact, or entertains the possibility of alternate methods. There is no time. Just do it! The notion that what you're doing isn't enough, isn't good enough, might even be harmful, is too frightening to consider because as a rule, it seems as if there is no other option.

I provided continuous care for Shirley for a long time. My husband and my son were there every day doing all they could. Her needs were endless. No matter which one of us was with her, I was the one who heard all the details of the day. Nothing was ever good enough. She never felt well. Her meals didn't please her. She had very little communication with the outside world. No one visited her and the phone calls were few and far between. Her complaints were constant and people tired quickly of the conversation. So, she couldn't wait for me to get home from work to talk with her.

I worked full time at a very demanding job and I have a family and a home to take care of. Trying to provide Shirley with the time she needed was exhausting. I knew it was too much. I knew it was stressful, but I couldn't see another path. I knew there would be a price to pay, but I didn't really think it might be the end of my life.

I was with Shirley all day on the

day she died. It's amazing to me how exhausting doing nothing can be. She was in the hospital and the nurses and therapists were performing most of the tasks Tom and I had been doing at home. At 7:55 she encouraged me to go home and have dinner. She'd been restless all day and fought with the nurses because she felt they didn't understand how sick she was. Throughout the day she kept repeating that she was dying but no one believed her. She was angry because people kept telling her she was "doing better". She told me to go home and get some rest. She said she was going to sleep for a while because she was tired and there was no point in my sitting there watching her sleep. She was scheduled to be discharged in the morning to a rehab facility. Within 15 minutes of my leaving, the hospital called Tom's cell phone to say mom died.

Just like that, it was over. I was busy trying to plan the revised caregiving schedule that would now be based on daily trips to the rehab center, and BAM!, it was all over.

All those hours we spent talking, day after day, night after night, and in the end, there were no words of "good-bye". I was pretty devastated. Despite all the time spent in preparation for the end, I wasn't really ready. I went onto automatic pilot and with my family and friends, I got through the closing ceremonies of caregiving. After it was all over, I began to feel exhausted. My family took me on a trip. I became increasingly more fatigued as we traveled and at one point, as I sat on the beach in Daytona Florida, I felt fairly certain it might be the last day of my life. In fact, I made it home the next day and went directly to my doctor's office where I went into cardiac arrest. I ended up in the

ICU of the local hospital. It was all pretty frightening. All my bodily systems were in crisis. My kidneys shut down, my heart was erratic, my oxygen levels were dangerously low. After a week in ICU I rebounded well. My systems were back in balance. I was physically exhausted and my body responded by collapsing. I was very lucky that I didn't die. I came close.

I experienced, first hand, the danger of unrelieved stress, a risk caregivers take every day.

If you can get some respite, have some time to regenerate yourself, options may appear. But even if you fail to have a creative moment as a result of respite, at least the respite will have enabled you to return to the usual tasks with renewed ability to perform them as well as your previous, best effort.

Getting Respite

How do you get respite? I've met very few caregivers who deny the benefit of respite, but most of the caregivers maintain that respite is impossible for them in their situation. I fully, and personally understand this concept, but I would like to say that many of the reasons offered about why respite isn't an option have to do with a lack of resources, but many, many others have to do with a decision to allow the care recipient to determine the conditions of care.

Caregiving, in our society, isn't a legal mandate. We don't require people to make personal sacrifices to care for others, even children. We expect parents to care for their children, but if the parent determines they don't want this responsibility any longer, they can turn their children over to the care and supervision of the state government. Being a caregiver, even a bad one, of a child is a choice. If you become pregnant and regret it, we allow you to give the child away. We don't stone you or imprison you. We recognize the importance of the voluntary nature of providing care and nurturance for another.

The same holds true when the roles reverse and we choose to become a caregiver for parents. It is a volitional act and it's essential that one remembers that fact. You can quit any time. You may not like the consequences, but you can walk away. You won't be forced to continue providing care. Once you acknowledge that your caregiving decision is in your control, you need to take charge of the care giving plan.

What are the circumstances under which you are willing to accept the role of caregiver. Part of the difficult emotional path of the caregiver is confronting the role reversal issue. One of the reasons it's important to face and accept it is that failure to do so will result in the care recipient unfairly controlling the care giving plan. Pretending that the care giving recipient is still the dominant one in the relationship will lead to the development of unreasonable care plans that place unnecessary burden on the care giver.

In caring for another it is part of basic human dignity to include the wishes and needs of the person for whom you're caring at the center of every decision that's made about care. However, considering what someone wants and the way they want it done doesn't trump everything else.

A caregiver, who is competent to engage in the decision process has an obligation to include the needs and abilities of the caregiver in the plan. The family caregiver isn't a paid professional who is doing this as a job. Caregiving is a love-based act of family and all participating members have to be included if the plan is to work. We can't sacrifice one for the sake of another. Everyone who chooses to be a part of the caregiving plan has to be a part of the compromise. No family caregiving plan is possible without compromise. Therefore, no plan should be approached with the expectation that everything that's done will be done exactly as dad wants it. It has to include the realities of caregiving: Who is available to execute the plan?

What competing pressures are on the caregivers? What are the physical, emotional and financial resources of the caregiver? What are the necessary components of the plan? What are the preferences of the care recipient? Are the abilities of the caregiver sufficient to the task? What resources does the care recipient bring to the plan?

I have participated in too many family meetings where the desire and demands of the care recipient were the only factors considered. Unreasonable fiats from the care recipient controlled the planning process. Caregivers were expected to perform all caregiving tasks even when there were multiple options to include in the plan that would have made the provision of care easier for the caregiver, and enabled the caregiver to provide care with less stress. Including adult daycare, once or twice a week can provide regularly scheduled rest for the caregiver and much needed separation between the caregiver and care recipient, with both feeling rejuvenated and glad to see each other when reunited after a day apart.

Using paid caregivers to help with challenging personal tasks such as bathing can be a great help in preventing caregiver stress caused by a strained back, and preventing care recipient stress by avoiding slips and falls in the bath. Using delivery services for groceries and pharmacy purchases can free the caregiver to spend better quality time visiting with the caregiver instead of rushing around performing endless errands. A monthly housecleaning service can keep the major household cleaning under control so the caregiver doesn't have to provide personal care, supervision and entertainment while also acting as housekeeper and washer woman.

Arranging for regularly scheduled visits, whether from a program such as a senior companion program or a church friendly visiting group, or just arranging for visits from family and friends on a social calendar, are essential to keep the care recipient stimulated and connected to life and to provide the caregiver with a bit of respite. These breaks in caregiving should be used to get away from caregiving responsibilities and refresh yourself. These are not visits when the caregiver becomes the entertainer and refreshment provider while the care recipient holds court as the hostess.

Unfortunately, none of these options are employed by many caregivers

because, "Dad won't go to day care."
"Mom won't let an aide bathe her."
Mom and Dad don't trust strangers in
their home." Mom doesn't want to
make conversation with people from
programs and church groups." "Dad
doesn't want nosey people he doesn't
know stopping by to check up on him."

Instead of exerting the power of the role
reversal – as you might have with your
kids who give you a laundry list of
reasons about why they didn't want to
go to school and you just turned around
and told them, there was no argument.
Just do it. You know it's essential to
their development to go to school and
you're the person in charge. You have
their best interest in mind and they're
going to school. – instead, you say, "I
know Dad would love daycare, they
have a great woodwork shop, and Dad
loves talking with other men about

woodworking but he doesn't want to go, so he'll be staying home." Home, bored, angry, and unhappy because he cannot see any options; he doesn't know how to plan for his day; and you've left him in charge of the caregiving plan.

The challenge to the adult child caregiver, and often the spousal caregiver is recognizing and accepting the change in your relationship with the care recipient. It means letting go of long held feelings of security provided through the relationship with the care recipient. Irrespective of the quality of the relationship with the care recipient, there exists in most of us a lingering sense of security which is tied to childhood memories of being cared for by our parents. They drove away the demons hiding in dark corners and comforted us. Although it may have been years, even decades since we called on them to save us from the bogeyman, somewhere, deep down, their capacity to provide safe harbor remains a force in our lives.

When we are asked, overtly or indirectly to become caregivers for our parents we step into the role of providing safe harbor instead of nestling into the longed for, safe harbor of home. If we fail to acknowledge that we have the responsibility to provide security, not just perform the tasks of daily living, we are denying the person we care for an integral component of care. Just as a mother who meets all the physical needs of her child but fails to establish an emotional connection, lacks the ability to soothe her child when in distress, so too, the caregiver's environment cannot provide the security the care recipient needs.

Although care recipients may fight adamantly to retain control over all decision making, in the same way a child will fight going off to bed even when exhausted, the care recipient will feel safer and ultimately more in control of him (her)self when a reasonable, caregiving plan is in place. Part of a reasonable plan has to include provisions for caregiver respite. If the caregiver is allowed to breakdown, the caregiving plan is bust and the care recipient is in jeopardy. Living in fear of that type of disruption places the care recipient in a precarious position. In that state the care recipient doesn't feel in control of self or plan. Acquiescing to a bad plan doesn't honor the will of the care recipient, it simply puts him in a bad place where eventually he'll have to face his frailty and inability to provide for himself. There is no honor or security in that care plan.

The caregiver has to deal with the issue head on. Include her needs in the plan as a condition of providing care. Initially there may be resistance, but ultimately it will result in a better plan where the needs of the care recipient can be met without sacrificing the caregiver.

I know a woman who was caring for her 91 year old, widowed mother. Her mom was mentally sharp and physically well but increasingly frail and unable to shop, cook, clean and generally maintain her home. She decided to move in with her unmarried daughter. The daughter did all the housework and supervision necessary. After a time, mom became accustomed to the presence of her daughter in the house and she didn't want her to go anywhere. She felt afraid to be left in the house alone. Initially, the daughter tried to honor her mother's wishes. She stayed at home with mom or she took mom with her when she went out. Day after day, week after week, month after month, they were inseparable. The daughter, an attractive, lively, recently retired professional became quiet, withdrawn and generally unhappy. She wanted to be a good daughter and be a caregiver but she also wanted a break from being a caregiver. She always enjoyed spending time with her mother whom she described as intelligent, interesting and informed, but now it was all such a rut. There was nothing new to talk about.

The suggestion was made to have mom go to the senior center a few days a week, but mom resisted, not wanting to be with a "bunch of old biddies", and the daughter shrugged and said "I can't make her go." The woman also had a son who lived out of state. After about a year of the mother and daughter living together, he came to visit. He saw his sister looking worn out and depressed and his mother argumentative and unhappy. He explored the resources in the community and came up with a plan for adult day care three times per week. He agreed to pay the cost of the program as his contribution to the caregiving needs of his mom. Mom resisted, but he insisted. He confronted mom with the obvious stress in the family and the toll it was taking on both mom and daughter. Because she was a rational woman who loved her daughter

she let go of her resistance and went
along with the son's plan. He laid out
the plan in a clear, reasonable way and
relied on the fact that they were a loving
family who ultimately wanted what was
best for everyone. Three times a week at
8:30 AM the adult day center mini-van
arrives to take mom out for the day and
at 4:30 they return her home. She has
so much to say about the program.
Some of it good and some of it critical
but none of it aimed at her daughter.
She shares stories about what happened,
who did what, what they ate and what's
planned for the next day.

Two days a week she goes to the senior
center. Her daughter takes her. Some
days the daughter stays and they do
things together. They're always
partnered in the monthly bridge

tournament and usually win. The
fondest moment for both of them came
when mom volunteered her daughter to
teach a line dance class to the 85+
group who wanted to dance but
couldn't keep up with the younger
seniors. Her daughter would do it she
said "because no one is more patient
and gentle with old biddies than she."

Accepting the role reversal, building a
safe secure harbor and ensuring she had
sufficient rest to be able to provide the
quality of care she wanted to give
enabled this caregiver to be a "fearless
caregiver".

5 WHERE'S THE GIFT?

Being given the opportunity to become a caregiver is a gift. You may say "If this is a gift, how would you describe a burden?" but, in fact, caregiving is a gift. Like all gifts however, it has to be unwrapped to be appreciated. One of the nicest, most useful gifts I ever received was a computer workstation/office that looked like a piece of fine furniture, but opened up to become an office unit that could be closed and locked away when not in use. It enabled me to maintain a formal dining room in a small house and have all my office-related needs in one convenient place. I loved it! But, when I received it, not so much. It was in a large, flat box about 5'X4'X4". I couldn't imagine what it was when I saw it under the Christmas tree, In fact, it was sort of annoying initially because it took up so much of the floor space, we could barely get to the other gifts on Christmas morning.

Once I unwrapped it and got a look at the photo of the contents I was mixed in my reaction. Obviously, a lot of assembly was required to turn the large box of parts into the beautiful cabinet in the photo. I am not handy. Assembly isn't my idea of fun. I always pay extra to have things assembled in the store. I hate reading the multi-language instructions and I always have too many parts left over when assembly is complete. Doors don't close properly, drawers don't slide smoothly and invariably, I nick and ding the finishes so it looks used before I get to use it. So, I had mixed feelings about this gift. My husband, the "gifter", has different feelings about assembly. For him, it's a contest between manufacturer and assembler and he, the assembler, will win.

And so, the office cabinet became the latest challenge to take over our dining room. On the very first day, setting the table for the holiday feast was made difficult as I had to navigate around the component parts spread around he dining room. He was so eager to begin assembly he had already begun categorizing the various parts. It was a time challenge. Every evening after dinner he would work on building the cabinet. It was a wonder. Articulating shelf to hold the key board, slide out file draws, printer shelf, nooks and cubbies for supplies, divided shelves for CDs, book shelves…such a wonder! Each piece had a "right" side and unfortunately, a "wrong" side. So, many times an entire section would be assembled and ready to be connected to the main structure when we would notice the "wrong" side was facing us. Disassemble! Start over. Was the cabinet really a gift? I never asked for it. It wasn't my idea. Why was it taking over my life? Evening after evening he worked on assembly. We couldn't use the dining room. I was climbing over completed file drawers and cubbies awaiting attachment. Would it ever end? Eventually, it was assembled, loaded with office supplies and is such a basic part of our home I can't imagine how we'd ever get along without it. But for a few weeks, in January, one year I thought it was a gift I wanted to return.

The same is often true about the gift of caregiving. It's never a gift you ask for. Often it's a gift you really don't want. It may not play to your strengths and you may not have natural talent for it, but there it is. You've got it and until you take the time to unwrap all the layers of it, look at it carefully, examine what it means to you and assemble a plan that works for you, you won't ever know what a gift it can be in your life. You hold the key to understanding and experiencing the gift of caregiving. The sooner you unwrap it and enable yourself to enjoy it, the easier your caregiver journey will be to navigate and the further you will travel on your path of personal development.

The Gift of Patience

"Patience is a virtue, catch it if you can, seldom found in woman, never found in man." I don't remember where or when I learned this little rhyme but I hear it playing on a loop in my brain whenever I hear the word patience. "Patience is a virtue". Why do we profess to value patience in our hurried lives? We don't really want to wait for anything. We want everything NOW and at warp speed. We can communicate with people the world over in a matter of minutes and yet were caught complaining about the speed of our Internet connection. We don't want to wait. We rush through Advent to get to Christmas as quickly as possible. We are in a hurry to get to the finish line. We don't often spend time enjoying the journey. We are eager to get to the endpoint. We hurry away childhood preparing for adulthood, as if our children won't become adults as a matter of natural development if we don't keep them on a preplanned timeline.

We admire the decisive, quick thinker. We criticize the slow learner. We become impatient with the checkout clerk who scans our items slowly. We complain about the server who moves too slow bringing us our meal. We demonstrate no interest in anything that requires patience, and yet we proclaim "Patience is a virtue". Why is there so little evidence of the virtue of patience in our lives?

One plausible reason may be the pressure we feel, every day, every waking moment to complete the tasks before us. We all have so many responsibilities. We wear so many hats. Even if we lower our standards and settle for "good enough" instead of striving to do our "best", we still feel further behind on a regular basis. We don't have the luxury of being patient. We're in too much of a hurry to "get it done".

The sense of hurry, hurry, doesn't lead us down a path of fulfillment. Have you ever heard anyone proclaim their pleasure and satisfaction over finishing life first; getting to their personal finish line before anyone? I doubt it. We tend to fantasize about long lives; we talk about long leisurely walks; we dream about restful spa vacations to restore our sense of balance. We know there is wisdom in seeking patience; were just in too much of a hurry to do it.

When we begin on a long term caregiver path with someone who is facing the rigors of aging or the terror of dying, we have to slow down. They are not in a hurry to be done. Even when there is pain and a desire for relief from the devastation of illness, there is also reluctance to end the journey. As caregivers, we can't hurry the process. There are many tasks necessary to complete in caring for another person. Some of them are very difficult, and on some level all of them are appreciated although often unacknowledged. However, the most important, most meaningful, and usually most difficult for the caregiver is to simply stay on the path with the care recipient and accompanying him/her toward the finish line with all the patience required to ensure the care recipient doesn't feel that you are rushing his/her life away.

You can't successfully fake patience. If you are thinking: "hurry, hurry, hurry, I have so many other things I have to do", the person you are caring for will read that in your body language, even if those words never reach your lips. I know a woman who is a very knowledgeable caregiver for her mother who had advancing dementia. She knows all the "right" things to say and what not to say to avoid making mom feel rushed. One day she was trying to get mom off to the day care center. This was one task in a day full of work, family and caregiver tasks to be accomplished. She was feeling pressured. She was trying to help mom get from the house to the car with as few distractions and unnecessary interruptions as possible. As they moved toward the car mom stopped in her tracks and said "You changed." It was an implied criticism which was dead right. She had changed. There were several new responsibilities in her life and she was feeling the pressure to respond to all of them and there wasn't enough time. Although she carefully monitored her words, mom could feel the sense of being rushed through her daughter's body language. She was no longer the incredibly patient person she had been before all the tasks piled up around her. Despite the dementia mom was aware of the changes. You can't fake patience. It's more than saying the right things. It's communicated as much through non-verbal behaviors as through words and actions. It requires the caregiver to be in the moment with the person they care for, sharing the experience.

You can control your words and your behavior will look calm and cool to everyone else, but the care recipient will know and in many ways, sometimes subtle, often overt, they will call you out on it. Most often we can recognize the awareness of feeling hurried in the caregiver through the changes in mood and affect they display. Care recipients will speak of feeling "like a burden", they'll look sad, their language will reveal feelings of depression, worthlessness and loss. The time and energy spent caring for a child is often much greater than that of caring for an elderly parent, but the child doesn't feel sad that (s)he' wasting your time; depressed that (s)he's so worthless you have to help with everything; guilty that you aren't caring for other parts of your life because you're caring for him/her.

In most cases there's a good degree of joy in caring for your child. You witness the growth and development of the miracle you've wrought. You delight in the almost daily changes as (s)he develops. Naturally, at times you're tired. The work is hard but rarely do you wish it was over or that it had never begun. Even when you hurry the child you are moving to the next exciting stage. So much life lays before the two of you. But in caring for an aging or dying loved one, most of life stretches behind you. If you hurry this stage, there will be no more. The person you love will be out of your life forever. Being able to slow down and experience the process together enables you to add to the collection of memories you possess. In the end, in life, our relationships are all memory collections, mental scrap books which we can open and revisit as desired.

When we care for someone we love, we want to do a good job and make the caring as beneficial as possible. That's why we do it. From love. So we want to slow down the process; share these moments; make new memories. We don't want it all to end with a sense of burden, loss and anger. How do we get to a place where we can provide the kind of loving caregiving we imagine? It's through the development of patience. One of the final steps in our adult development is the development of patience. We have the capacity to develop patience throughout our lifetime, but it isn't until later in life that most of us begin to work on the development of this virtue.

There are several things that have to come together to successfully develop patience. We have to have an ability to feel empathy. So often we are trying to be patient with another person who is exhibiting behavior that isn't precisely the behavior we would prefer. If we can empathize with them, have an understanding of who they are, their strengths and limitations, we are more able to feel the difficulty they are having accomplishing a task in the way we want it done. We are then able to wait, patiently for them to succeed.

We also need to have experience with a range of life situations. Experience also enables us to understand the difficulty involved in tasks and allows us to be patient as someone executes a task.

Lastly, we need to have reached the stage in our development where we feel we have accomplished some of the major milestones in our life and are ready to refine our personal development. The big rocks are in place, the foundation is set and now we smooth out the rough edges, Here is the opportunity to develop the virtue of patience.

If you are caring for someone, and truly providing them with all they need, you will spend significant time just being with them. Not *doing* things for them, although there is much doing, but simply *being*. Occupying time and space together. Sharing a closeness that can't be phoned-in. It's genuine, time consuming and requires patience. You become better at "being" through the practice of caregiving. If you're like most people in our society you're too busy "doing" to stop and allow yourself the time to experience "being".

As you sit with someone you're caring for there may be many moments of quiet. Who knows what you'll think during those moments. Recollections, dreams, plans, past hurts, tears, so much can bubble up when we have quiet time to sit and just "be". Initially, it's difficult. There's so much to do and you're just sitting, wasting precious time. But really, this is the precious time. The time to be together. Perhaps, one of the last times.

If the daily tasks of caregiving, combines with all the other tasks of daily life are so great that there truly isn't any time to just be, then you need to get/accept help with the other tasks. The number one task of caregiving should be helping the person you care for feel loved, treasured. Someone you want to be with. Someone you want to spend time with. Not just the object of your efforts, in the way you care for your vacationing neighbor's pet pooch.

Once you design a reasonable caregiver plan with appropriate respite built in, and you accept help with some of the tasks, you can begin to experience the personal growth and development that will occur as you sit and share the end stages of the life of another who has known you intimately.

Memories will arise and new light will be shed on the past. Secrets will be shared. Adult perspective will be applied to childhood memories and new perspectives will be formed. Throughout the experience you will become more of yourself. You will develop greater self-awareness which will enable you to have greater understanding and patience with others.

The gift of patience isn't bestowed on you, but through caregiving, the opportunity to develop patience is revealed. Once you've developed the capacity for patience, the next developmental stage in your adult life will begin.

The Expansion of Empathy

"I feel so sorry for you" is an expression of sympathy. It conveys to the person hearing your words that you care about them and you take pity on them and the situation in which they find themselves. Contrast that with former President Clinton's convincingly expressed "I feel your pain". Feeling another person's pain is an expression of empathy. It says to the listener "I understand your situation; I know your pain" How can we know another person's pain? Through personal experience. The speaker of these words is sharing with the listener a message about shared experience. When we share a common experience we are less likely to be critical and judgmental. We understand how difficult a particular life experience can be. We understand it through first hand experience. We know the difficulty in facing challenging decisions; the pain of making unpopular choices; the fear of making wrong decisions.

The empathetic response is akin to placing an arm around the listener and saying" It's OK. I don't judge you. You can share your burden with me." None of these words need to be spoken. The empathy expressed in the acknowledgement of the shared experience is sufficient to support the listener. This is the concept behind self help programs built on the AAA model, people, who themselves are in recovery, sharing their experience with others. In so doing, they reinforce their own recovery and provide support to others who often feel the pain of criticism and judgment from those who take pity on them. They want to support them, but they fail miserably in their attempts.

Pity creates a divide between the person being pitied and the person expressing feelings of sorrow. When I pity you I am also, silently, saying, " You have a problem that's causing you pain...and I don't. I'm up here and you're down there. I'm in control of my life situation and you're not. I have power and you're weak." When people are feeling low-down, powerless, out of control, they don't want to be reminded. They want to retain a semblance of self control and personal authority. Therefore, there's a strong tendency to reject expressions of support from well intended people when they are delivered as expressions of sympathy.

The development of empathy comes with a price. One can be aware of the value of empathy and can learn language that is less full of pity, and more supportive, but empathetic expressions are more than a learned academic exercise. Empathy develops within an individual as they pass through the stages of life and get their share of bumps and bruises. Everyone gets bumped on the head a few time before reaching the end of their lives. Not everyone learns lessons from their life experiences. For some, it takes decades before the light dawns. When we speak of the "wisdom" of aging, as most cultures do, it is the development of empathy that undergirds the wisdom. After living a long time and after having innumerable life experiences, the wise older person understands what you are experiencing. They have been there and have had similar feelings.

Unfortunately, one of the sad facts of aging is that by the time the older person has an accumulation of life experiences to share, their ideas and opinions are often deemed irrelevant and shuttled aside. But, not always. One of the most beautiful relationships in Western culture is between grandparents and grandchildren. There is an intimacy and feeling of love, affection and support that is unlike any other. The grandparent can convey an understanding of the feelings of the grandchild that is truly personal and connected to their own past. Often, parents are too busy with daily life errands to pay close attention to the "silly" concerns of their children. Issues, such as where to sit in the school cafeteria, or what color crayon to use when making a pre-K self-portrait, just don't warrant the time and attention of busy parents as they try to work full-time, maintain a household, serve as family chauffer, shopper, plumber, handyman, launderer, and sometimes, caregiver to grandma or grandpa.

For many children, grandparents are eager to listen to their concerns, and with the luxury of a slower pace of life they can reflect on their own experiences. The technology of life has changed big time, but the pain and challenges of personal development have not. Children are still trying to determine who they are. They're trying to fit into peer groups. They're testing the boundaries around them and seeking greater independence while also longing to be cared for by mom and dad. Their bodies are developing. Hormones still rage and the pursuit of a date for the school dance hasn't changed. Grandma understands that on the deepest level of empathy.

It isn't the presents that Nana and Poppy buy their grandchildren that makes them so connected to the children. Long distance grandparents who send fabulously expensive gifts may be appreciated but they are not connected in the way grandma who is home to meet the school bus is. It is the shared, empathetic experience in which grandma can communicate to grandchild: "I'm here. I understand. I feel your pain and joy."

Fulfillment of Selflessness

When you look at another person and ask yourself "What does she need? What can I do to help him?" you are having selfless thoughts. By contrast, when your thoughts are dominated by concerns of "What's in it for me? Why do I have to do this? Why does she always call me?" you are having self-centered thoughts. There isn't a right or a wrong way to think. Our thoughts reflect our feelings. We're entitled to our feelings. They develop out of a lifetime of experiences and relationships. However, as we develop and evolve as people, over time, we begin to develop the capacity to see things from another person's perspective. Using our empathetic skills we feel the experience of others, not simply the awareness of their situation, but the affective component. We know what they're feeling. We understand what a particular event means to them.

This enables us to remove ourselves from the picture and fully see the situation as it impacts on the other person. It helps us answer the question "Why did she do that?", which arises so often when we witness the behavior of another person. If I am in the picture, I am evaluating what I see in terms of how it impacts me, and perhaps, how it impacts the other person.

But, if I am removed from the picture I can fully see the behavior from the perspective of the other person. Its impact on me isn't an issue, therefore, I am able to be impartial. My reaction is fully based on the feelings or circumstances of the other. This is not a skill that develops quickly or easily. We are accustomed to evaluating behavior as it affects us. It is part of our self-preservation instinct. If we aren't watching out for ourselves, who is? When we're concerned with self-preservation, we run the risk of stunting our growth. Our personal development is limited by our concern with keeping what we have. It is only when we're willing to take a risk and perhaps lose something we think we have, that we discover what could be. We possess the capacity to be more loving, kinder, more compassionate, but we have to be willing to risk self-preservation to find the satisfaction in selflessness.

If you think about your daily activities, what are the activities that bring you the greatest satisfaction? For most people, when they answer this question, they discover that helping others, serving others, spending time with loved ones, feeling like they make a difference in someone's life, are the actions that bring them joy. In all these activities the focus is away from the self and toward the needs of others.

Does this mean that caregivers should deny their own needs? Only serve others? Ignore their own feelings? NO! Placing oneself in jeopardy, physically or emotionally, only results in catastrophic situations where all attention is eventually drawn to the caregiver. Caregiver failing to care for self is perhaps the ultimate act of selfishness since the caregiver who self- destructs leaves everyone else behind. Rather, the selfless caregiver must care for self in a manner that ensures the caregiver will be able to continue in the role of caregiver for as long as needed.

When you travel by airplane and the flight attendant instructs you in the use of in-flight oxygen. They remind you that if you're traveling with children, *i.e.* someone for whom you're providing care, place the oxygen mask over your face and nose first, before you attend to the needs of the kids. Initially I interpreted this instruction to mean that children had less need for oxygen. Why else would you delay getting oxygen to a

defenseless child? Because that
defenseless, dependent child is
dependent on the caregiver. So, the
caregiver has to be able to provide care.
They have to have sufficient oxygen in
their blood stream to ensure that they
are able to rescue the child in an
emergency. The same holds true every
day and in every situation for all
caregivers. As long as someone is
dependent on you, you have to ensure
your basic needs are being tended to or
you won't be able to care for the needs
of another. Caring for one's health,
getting respite, maintaining social
relationships are essential acts if
caregivers are to perform as effective
caregivers over a prolonged period of
time.

I met a woman at a caregiver support
group for caregiver spouses one
evening. She was talking about an

incident in her life and she revealed that
her husband was unable to leave the
house independently, used a wheelchair
for mobility and spent most of his time
at home. She worked fulltime and was
out of the house about 10 hours a day.
The thought crossed my mind that he
probably was eager for her return each
day to have someone to talk to and
bring the outside world into his life. I
wondered if he resented her going out
to the support group and leaving him
home. I also wondered if her going out
without him was selfish. I imagined
myself in his position and felt that I'd
resent it. I couldn't get up and go out
anytime I felt like it, why should she?
Perhaps my eyes revealed my feelings
because, unsolicited she began to talk
about what a difficult decision it was for
her to join the support group. She
wrestled with the fact that she'd be

going out without him and feared he feel that she was trying to get away from him. That she didn't want to spend time with him. That his illness had created a crack in their relationships that was going to spread.

So, why did she join the support group? She recognized that she had a mix of feelings and fears related to his illness and the progression of her role as a caregiver, and she had nowhere to express those feelings. Family and friends couldn't understand her feelings or fears on the same level as she, having never experienced them. Her husband, perhaps, shared the same feelings but she didn't want to share all her worries, fears and especially her frustration and anger with him, for fear he would feel guilty about something he couldn't control. She needed to talk with people who really understood her situation and were willing to just listen and not judge.

Sharing her feelings and not being judged enables her to go home after a group meeting feeling refreshed. She knows why she's a caregiver and she's in it for the long haul. She loves her husband, but she gets tired. She feels angry that their lives were tossed upside down by his disease. She hates the fact that the simplest things that they used to do now require effort and planning. However, she feels capable of doing what needs to be done because of the support she feels from her support group. A selfish response to her caregiver demands might have been to call it quits on the marriage, but also, selfishly, she might have stayed in the marriage and caregiver role filled with unrelieved anger and sadness until she finally became ill and was relieved of her caregiving role. Sometimes, the martyred type of caregiving looks selfless but it isn't because it results in the care recipient being left without care, or feeling guilty for needing care.

The caregiver has to be concerned about long range plans for the care recipient. Looking down a long term path means ensuring the caregiver will be there for the care recipient. The care recipient needs to go to sleep at night knowing that the safe harbor of care is surrounding him. That doesn't happen if the caregiver is in jeopardy. For this caregiver, the most selfless thing she could have done was to find a way to get support for her feelings and relief from her anger, without projecting them onto her husband. She comes home from the support group feeling lighter. Unexpressed feelings are a heavy weight to carry around in one's heart. Once spoken, discharged into the air, we can feel free from them. Especially when someone hearing your words can say " I know what you mean. I feel the same way. I always thought it was just me."

Being willing to take a good look at yourself, get feedback from others, ensure you have a plan in place to keep yourself supported through challenging periods are difficult but necessary actions to keep a caregiver going. The beauty of it however, is that in so doing you are developing skills and insight that will serve you throughout the remainder of your life.

As we age we continue to develop throughout the entire life cycle. At each step we face challenges that are also opportunities for growth and development. In the earliest stage of life, our development is driven primarily by biology. Our physical development is preeminent, but as adults, development takes a more internal course. We expand as individuals. Our character becomes preeminent.

We move from early life where development is focused on the ability to master the external world to later life where development is focused on the internal life of spirit which enables us to live together as people and nurture the development of others. Not everyone masters this stage of life. Switching the physical, competitive, external world to the internal, contemplative world requires the ability to be selfless. If one remains focused exclusively on self and mastery, which leads to thoughts such as "I can do it better than you.", "I'm smarter than you." I'm more productive than you.", then one doesn't experience the sense of satisfaction and freedom that comes with development in the next stage of life.

Caregivers' selfless acts require them to put themselves in the care recipients' place, to feel the situation from the care recipient's perspective, to put the needs and wishes of the care recipient front and center in all caregiving tasks. Learning to ensure that the care recipients needs and feelings are addressed and not just that the physical tasks of caregiving are performed from a check list is an important skill in the development of selflessness. Most people don't know how to do this when they first become care givers. There are many stories caregivers share about mistakes they made in the early steps of a caregiving journey by having a checklist of things needing to be accomplished. Caregivers check off each item with great efficiency but never "satisfy" the care recipient.

I remember helping to care for my father after he had a stroke. I dutifully arrived at his apartment with my cleaning supplies, prepared to clean the kitchen and bath, run the dishwasher, wash and dry a load of clothes and cook a pot of soup. I had my list figured to the minute. But , each time, my father wanted a pot of tea, and he wanted to talk. I'd spend the evening and leave feeling like a failure because the house wasn't as neat as I wanted it to be when the visiting nurse came. He on the other hand remembered those visits as a great success. I satisfied his list of wants and needs for affiliation and attention. Those tasks never made my list, but were as important to him as a clean kitchen floor. If I didn't stop cleaning and share a cup of tea with him, I could have completed my list but he would have been unhappy and unsatisfied which surely would have displayed itself as anger and depression.

Learning to negotiate the balance between what someone wants (internal) and what they need (external) is an art. When someone is good at it, they become very effective leaders and negotiators.

We talk on the level of our heads. We say what we obviously know is the "right thing" to say, but we function on the level of the heart. In the end, when push comes to shove we act on our feelings. We even say things like" I know I should..., but I just have to..." Being able to recognize the feelings behind another's words and helping them design a plan that honors those feelings and not just ideas, will make

you an effective planner. The things
you plan will have greater likelihood of
happening because the feelings of the
people you planned with are included in
the plan. The feelings are the things
that cause the implementers of any plan
to undermine the plan. For example, we
meet and all agree that the most
efficient way to handle the shortage of
staff to provide one-to-one counseling is
to cut back on the number of people we
assist. Therefore, we agree we'll only
see 10 people per day. So we begin to
implement the plan but 12 people come
in and ask for help. They're all very
much in need of help. The counselor
doesn't like to say no to anyone. She
feels her sense of herself is tied to her
willingness to help. She wants to be
thought of as a caring, compassionate
person. That image doesn't jibe with
saying "I can't help you." to people who

seek her out. So, she agrees to see them during her lunch hour. She's keeping to the planned schedule and she's keeping her personal mission in-tact. But, the next day more people come and she has the same inner conflict. So, she tells them to come back and see her after hours. She stays late to see them. But more people come so she has them come back the following day before the work day starts. The plan, designed to ensure the counselors are not being overwhelmed by the growing demand for service has been corrupted by the very people it was designed to protect. It failed because it didn't address the feelings of the counselors. The counselors didn't express their feelings because the plan seemed so logical, and obviously needed, that they would have appeared foolhardy to counter it. But, once in practice, feelings overtook the

situation and the plan, designed to
minimize stress became a factor in
increasing stress.

Taken to its logical conclusion, in this
case the counselor would have
continued in this manner for a time,
become overwhelmed and "burnt-out"
and quit, leaving no one to help any of
the clients, about whom she cared so
much. If the planner could have been
more in touch with the feelings of
others, if the selfish need to control by
making a plan without understanding
the internal needs of everyone
concerned, the situation might have
gone very differently. Burn out could
have been avoided.

Caregivers learn this lesson early if they
are caring for someone with strongly
held feelings. For others it may happen
more slowly if the care recipient tries to

accommodate to plans to simplify life for the caregiver. Eventually however, the caregiver begins to recognize the value of care given selflessly versus the value of care given selfishly.

The growing capacity to provide selfless care seen in caregivers is carried over into other aspects of life, beyond the caregiver role. The person who is aware of the needs of others, and who is willing and able to act in response to those needs, without focusing on his/her own needs will be a very effective communicator, negotiator and leader because that caregiver has the ability to see what a situation calls for to satisfy the true needs of people .

The combination of empathy, which enables us to understand or experience the feelings of another and selflessness which empowers us to put personal needs aside and act in the way another wants us to act, creates a circumstance destined to gratify the needs of the other. If I truly feel what you need and want, and I am willing to address that need in the way you want, rather than the way I think is best for you, I am certain to please you.

You might reasonably ask, does acting on someone's feelings and doing what they want ensure their needs are met? Perhaps they have an unrealistic view of their abilities or a simplistic understanding of their problems. Although acting on the feelings and preferences of a person may lead to a flawed action plan, failure to make feelings and desires central to a plan guarantees failure. Why? Because our goal as caregivers is to provide care. Care has outcomes associated with it that include the care recipient's feeling that the plan reflects them and their wishes. It is based on the feelings of the care recipient. If the care recipient doesn't feel central to the plan of care, everything that flows from the plan is problematic. The care recipient feels devalued; self-esteem is crushed; motivation to participate in the plan is nil. When a care recipient doesn't feel (s)he is the center of the plan, and (s)he experiences the above reactions, (s)he then lacks the ability to fully cooperate with the plan.

If a care recipient has an illness that requires a therapeutic treatment plan that is painful, arduous and riddled with side effects, the motivation of the care recipient to complete the plan of care, and the efficacy of the treatment, is greatly impacted by the decision to seek treatment. If the care recipient wants aggressive treatment, no stone left

unturned, fight to the end, facing
difficult treatment, the caregiver can be
at the side of the loved one, providing
support through transportation to
treatments, comfort and care after
treatment, advocacy in the treatment
setting and words of encouragement
and prayer when it gets difficult. This is
the choice the care recipient made and
the caregiver is there to support that
choice. Although both the caregiver
and care recipient may experience
discouragement, doubt or even regret
about the choice, there is little conflict
that arises in the caregiver-care recipient
relationship because the choice was
made by the care recipient. When
options are provided and free choices
are made, implicit in that dynamic is the
fact that changes can be made. The care
recipient can opt out of the plan; can
reevaluate the cost/benefit equation and

determine it's not worth the effort to continue with the plan. This sense of possibility, freedom of choice, is empowering to the care recipient. At a time in life when power is being drained away by age and illness, being central to the planning and decision making is affirming of one's status as an adult.

Creating a situation in which someone has the opportunity to select a path which may create increased burden on oneself requires selflessness. As long as the caregiver's focus is on the caregiver's preference, rather than the care recipient's preference, there is the strong likelihood that the plan that evolves will be met with resistance. The caregiver should make his/her feelings known and part of the care recipient's choices must include consideration of the care giver's capacity to support the care recipient. However, ironically, in placing the care recipient's preferences above the caregiver's preferences, in this manner, the caregiver will experience less resistance from the care recipient and an enhanced sense of accomplishment in the role of caregiver.

It isn't a manipulation. The caregiver can't pretend to allow the care recipient to make choices, provide lip service to including the care recipient's preferences in the plan, while planning how to get the care recipient to make the choices the caregiver is certain are "best" for the care recipient. This approach disrespects the care recipient. Some of us are powerful debaters and can construct a scenario with which only a fool would openly disagree, but when agreement with the plan comes about by winning a debate, rather than through listening and trying to hear the feelings of the care recipient, the plan fails to meet the goal of providing care. It may result in achieving the completion of any number of tasks, but it will not lead to a deepening of the relationship between the caregiver and the care recipient. It won't enable the care recipient to feel enveloped in a snug harbor of love. It won't enrich the development of the caregiver. The gift of caring isn't unwrapped and the enrichment it can provide isn't experienced. Sadly, for some, instead of benefitting from the gift, the caregiver is left with feelings of regret and bitterness.

Increase in the Capacity to Love

Ultimately, love is what we seek. To love, and be loved is the greatest joy we experience. The urge to love is basic and exists on all levels of our lives: spiritual, emotional, cognitive and physical. It washes over us in waves of ecstasy. It moves us to accomplish seemingly impossible acts. It connects us to the grand world around us and grounds us in the intimate relationships in which we live our day to day lives. And the "greatest of these is love". It is the greatest gift we can give and it's the greatest gift we can receive. When we are very lucky, we give and receive simultaneously.

Caregiving creates the opportunity to give and receive love simultaneously. When we give unselfishly of ourselves to care for others, they receive that generous act as a gift of love, freely given. This moves the care recipient to mirror back the caregiver's love with love for the caregiver. Parents provide care for children for years. It's a requirement of the role of parent . It is an expectation by society of parents.

Although it is the basis for developing our initial sense of love, it isn't always experienced as a mutual, simultaneous love. Kids expect to be cared for. "It's your job to care for me, Mom! I didn't ask to be born!" Words often heard by parents. Kids will learn to love from the experiences they have being cared for by parents, but it will be years to come before the mutually shared love will be expressed between them. On the other hand, there are no requirements of caregivers of adults. Whether it's spouse, parent or sibling, our acts of caring are actions of free will. The more we exercise free will in selfless acts, the more we increase our capacity to love. Our hearts open to the care recipient as our empathetic, selfless feelings determine our actions. The care recipient experiences the action as freely given, empathic and selfless and is moved to feel and express love.

This is one of the reasons that the caregiver has to remain mindful of the fact that caregiving is an option (s)he's selected at this point in life and like all optional actions can be stopped at any time. The free, selfless choice that the caregiver makes, to care for another, rather than the actual task itself, is what moves the care recipient to feel and express love. If the caregiver wants to provide care, and not just complete tasks, then it is essential to remain mindful of the purpose of caring and the free choice it constitutes. When you opt to spend your time and talent, ensuring the care and comfort of another, that action is love. Love inspires love.

The more care we provide in this
manner, the more we expose ourselves
to love. Love is a powerful,
empowering feeling that strengthens our
resolve. When we are transmitting love
we experience self-satisfaction. We feel
we've "done the right thing". We're
happy we were able to meet the needs
of someone we care for. Even if love
isn't returned by the care recipient, it is
reflected in the universe and improves
the environment around us. Who,
among, us would object to being
described as "loving", "caring", or
"giving"? Caregiving offers the
opportunity, on a daily basis to
experience the act of loving. If you're a
caregiver, you may be so immersed in
the tasks of caring that the gift goes
unnoticed. Look around and see the
woman a few doors down the block
who lives her life without the "burden"

of caregiving. She's alone, never married, no kids, parents are dead. She goes to work every day, has a cat and a dog for company and she knits and quilts for hobbies. She has a lot of love to give, but it's unexpressed. She doesn't have the opportunity to share her love. You may feel she's excessively concerned with her pets, but the urge to love is so strong, it has to be expressed somewhere. We develop our ability to love and feel love through our expression of love for another.

The caregiver has been given an opportunity to expand the capacity for love and the possibility of receiving love simultaneously. These experiences provide an immediate feeling of joy, and expand the future potential to love and receive love from others. So often, in life, our relationships are confounded by the complexities of life. Although we

love many people around us we often
feel the conflict and crises in our lives
suppress our feelings of love. Instead,
tension, anger, resentment, fear and
frustration characterize key relationships
in lives. For many, life ends without
ever redressing these feelings. We fail to
experience the pure joy that comes with
loving relationships and miss the
opportunity to grow in our capacity to
love.

When the caregiver enters into a
caregiving relationship (s)he is given the
opportunity to confront old feelings, to
examine adult relationships, to bring
mature understanding to incidents
carried over from childhood. A new
appreciation and understanding of the
care recipient and the caregiver is
possible. Healing old wounds and
forgiving in the caregiver relationship
will lead to expansion of the caregiver's

capacity to love in other relationships as well.

Seeing the care recipient in a new light, adult, freed from childhood expectations and parental disappointments can facilitate the deepening relationship between caregiver and care recipient. Both arrive at a new level of appreciation for each other and experience a joy in the relationship that enhances the lives of both eternally.

ABOUT THE AUTHOR

Dr. Kidder is a social worker who worked 27 years as a medical social worker in a community hospital. For the past 14 years she's been the director of the Aging & Disability Resource Center of the Agency on Aging of South Central CT. In addition, she's taught part-time at several colleges and universities as an adjunct instructor and is currently a member of the faculty at the University of New Haven, teaching Aging Policy.

Dr. Kidder has extensive experience working with family caregivers, but her primary experience in caregiving, which lead to the writing of this book, was as a caregiver for her mother. Through that experience she discovered the *Gift of Caregiving*.

Made in the USA
Charleston, SC
11 June 2014